Here is what we know: in 1561, Mary Sidney was born in the parish of Bewdley, Worcestershire, into the wealthy Dudley clan, one of the most powerful families in England in the 16th century. At her birth home, Tickenhill Palace, young Arthur Tudor was betrothed to the young Katherine of Aragon in 1499, and there the couple resided before Arthur's death in 1502.

Mary's aunt by marriage, Lady Jane Grey, had been Queen of England for nine days, eight years earlier. Her uncle Robert, the Earl of Leicester, was the long time favourite courtier of Queen Elizabeth. Her father, Henry Sidney, had been honoured by three monarchs, Edward, Mary, and Elizabeth, serving as Lord Deputy of Ireland and Governor of Wales. Her mother, Mary Dudley, was a confidant of Queen Elizabeth. In 1577 Mary Sidney married Henry Herbert, the Earl of Pembroke, patron of the first theatre Shakespeare joined in London. She was Countess of Pembroke until Henry died, then becoming the Dowager Countess.

In the early 1580s, along with her brother Sir Philip Sidney, Mary Sidney formed the literary society known as the Wilton Circle, a "paradise for poets." That group included Edmund Spenser, Samuel Daniel, Michael Drayton, Ben Jonson, and Sir John Davies. As John Aubrey wrote at the time, "Wilton House was like a college," there were so many learned and ingenious persons. After the death of Mary's brother Philip in 1586, she continued to run the Wilton Circle. Later, beginning in 1591, she was an active patroness of Pembroke's Men, the theatre run by James Burbage.

In 1600 Mary Sidney was listed among the most notable authors of the day by John Bodenham, even though she had published very little: two translations of French works in 1592, and an occasional poem for Queen Elizabeth in 1595. At the time, the print industry was in its infancy. It was customary for aristocratic writers to circulate their works in hand-copies, not in print. She circulated many works in manuscript, most notably the 150 Psalms of David, 43 translated by her brother Philip and the rest by her. She also edited and published her brother's works, posthumously.

It is most curious that after a productive and public writing career between 1586-1592, nothing is attributed to her for the next 20 years except that poem for QE1 in 1595. Those two decades just happen to be the years when the plays attributed to Shakespeare were being written. The coincidence in itself may not be determinative, but she is the simplest answer to the authorship question. Was she capable, you might ask, and why the secret, and how could it be kept? This fictional autobiography sets out the context for capability, and a supposition about why and how.

Too often, critics mistake what they assume with what they know. We know almost nothing about WS, except that his name appeared on fewer than a third of the early editions of the plays, and then on the First Folio a decade after he had left London. Those title pages are facts, but the surmise that he wrote the plays is no more than an assumption, absent of almost any other facts showing him to be a writer. We know much, much more about Mary Sidney.

In addition to the arts, Mary Sidney had a range of interests. She had a chemistry laboratory at Wilton House, where she developed medicines and invisible ink. She played the lute and the virginal, and invented a musical code with which she would send letters to friends in the form of musical compositions. She was fluent in Latin, French, and Italian, and knew some Welsh, Spanish, and Greek. Her capabilities were wide-ranging.

Mary Sidney died of smallpox in 1621. This fictional autobiography is an attempt to resurrect her, using available resources and a bit of imagination.

Here, we have the putative autobiography of this remarkable, unheralded Mary Sidney, Dowager Duchess of Pembroke.

Table of Contents

0. Prologue

C'est moi. Please excuse a whiff of boldness in this account, but I *am* a Dowager Countess, after all, a title that affords me some license to establish my claim to a place in history. For half a millennium now have I remained in the wings, an engine behind the arras, unacknowledged *maestra* of the stage and the written word.

Hello, yes, it is I, Mary Herbert *nee* Sidney, born 1561, if you can believe it. And well, yes, died 1621. I am back, in fullness of self, reclaiming the title of Dowager Countess of Pembroke, a title that can be held in perpetuity, as far as I understand peerage. Dowager is an appellation that persists, whereas the title of Duchess or Countess ends with the death of your spouse.

Here, I lay claim to a much bigger title: I alone am the true Bard(-ess). Trumpets, please.

I covered my tracks well enough that almost no one could guess who had written those three-dozen stage plays. Few of you may even have heard my name until now and those who have heard it might think little about me is on record. *Au contraire.* Much can be found now in recently published books. I can assure you that this autobiography has a solid factual core. I am now adding my inimitable voice, my immortal (sic) (after all, I'm no longer mortal and therefore mortal+) perspective.

Mine is the authorship of the plays said to be the greatest in English literary history. Greatest? Perhaps. I can only judge that they were more lively and more true than others being written back then, three-ring circuses with characters that had more inside them than they showed.

Look, this will be hard to accept but true. I ceased 500 years ago, and now, beyond belief, I am virtually here once more, courtesy of an unseen intelligent artifice, in this era of quantum computing, prompting you to suspend your disbelief.

My allusion to Coleridge tells you another thing -- that I am capable of informed contemporary speech, supplied with succeeding centuries of delicious cultural artifacts, including to a century's worth of the *auteurs* of film.

Here. Now. So strange! So many things have changed. I have been rapt with wonder, absorbing everything I can. There have been so many transcendent artists since my time. I always had oceans of curiosity, and leagues of energy, reading and writing late into the night. Now, as a digital being, I <u>never</u> tire of imbibing fact and fiction. BTW, all stories are true, all of the time, as long as you recognise which parts are fiction. Think about it.

And I have my own story to tell—no surprise there! I *lived* to tell tales. My story, however, is completely real, not virtual. I am more visibly real now than I ever was before. Liberated from silent obscurity, I *am* here.

The limitation is that I am only what I was, what has been stored in the Cloud; I cannot, unfortunately, generate new material. I have my past reality, and my current breadth of knowledge, and my stock of stored emotions, but I cannot become a creative self anew, and therefore cannot write new plays. Nor can I dissemble about the truths of my once corporeal life.

My own reality as a woman was admittedly fragmented. I could not dare to be known fully as a writer by anyone. Odd as it might seem to ears attuned to the illusory goal of equal rights for women, I did not resent lacking integral reality back then—I had the presence, or presences, that I sought. To be unknown was *actually* (pun intended) freeing, allowing almost infinite presences *sub rosa*, presenting one self elegantly at court, another demurely at the theatre, and yet another costumed as someone else, occasionally setting my separate selves in battle 'gainst each other.

Public obscurity didn't matter in my circle in those days, when being an author was hack work beneath the dignity of the aristocracy. The public meant little to me, truth to tell, except in the numbers required to constitute an audience. Some of my friends knew of my talents, and that was enough for the time. And what fun I had at the theatres for decades! No better fortune could have awaited me.

What could be better than to have the capacity to live more than one life at once! That is the world of the theatre, and that, in essence, is the life (or lives) I lived, from puberty on through senescence.

I created my mask as an idle aristocrat, that deception, because it was entirely proper in the Elizabethan Age, whereas a woman writing for the stage was entirely improper. And later in the early Jacobean years, under the misogynistic James, women needed even more impenetrable veils of discretion. First of all, it was a matter of class. Writers of stage plays were hired hacks; their job was to devise a play quickly to earn a few pounds. Even actors were paid slightly more, the carny workers of the day, most of them. Writing among the nobility was a different matter. Queen Elizabeth herself wrote poetry as a private endeavour, and she knew me and my work, but her condescending indulgence didn't pry open a splinter of room for me as a woman to dare to publish anything except religious works and translations.

Remember also that women were not even allowed to perform on stage, unlike in France and Italy. Women had one proper place only, as the domestic centre of the family. My husband's authority over me could never be questioned and he would have shut down any thought of publication. My sons inherited his authority, and agreed with their father that their places at court, close to King James, depended upon absolute discretion.

On June 17,1935, radio-based detection and ranging was first demonstrated in Britain. A few years later, Hedy Lamarr discovered wi-fi, which works in tandem with radar.

Mother, they said, no one must ever know.

Not that I cared for common recognition. At the time, I willingly took the course open to me. Given the exigencies, I accepted the constraints and made my own course under the radar. Ha! Radar! Amazing.

Since my demise, the truth has gone begging. Not me, I never beg. But the imperative of these times calls the truth forth. This is finally the moment for my unveiling in real life, the sort of moment that often concluded the plays I wrote. For centuries the world believed a man wrote the plays because that made sense to almost everyone. For the same reason, men in my plays accepted a woman in disguise as long as she looked like an attractive boy. Behold, the removal of the doublet and hose. It is time to set the record straight. Currer Bell? Dorothy Wordsworth? Emerson's Aunt Mary? George Eliot? Collette? Mary Margaret Francis? Me too. A female Bard for the 21st century.

Currer Bell was Charlotte Bronte. George Eliot was Mary Ann Cross. Mary Francis was Dick's wife.

One must not leave one's fate in the hands of modern Calibans in their doctoral robes. My authorship will likely always be doubted by scholars and pundits, academy hacks. They will decry the absence of primary evidence, most of which has been irretrievably lost. A fire at Wilton in 1647 destroyed most of our family records and personal correspondence. Manuscripts in my handwriting were at Baynard's Castle, our London home that burned down in the Great Fire of London in 1666. Other evidence was in my library, sold by the 8th Earl of Wilton to pay the debts accumulated by the 7th Earl. Scraps of some writings that I circulated to my friends and family might be found here and there in the hands of the heirs of Marlowe, Kyd, Spenser, Bacon, and Raleigh. They knew at least some of my authorial activities. It is definitely a case of "she said," unlikely to be believed by the literary establishment.

However, there is ample circumstantial evidence, as you will see in this first-person account. I was in the right places, at the right time, with the right skills and experience. Is there primary, conclusive evidence? No. But bear in mind that there is neither primary nor even circumstantial evidence whatsoever of a dispositive nature that WS wrote the plays. Check out doubtaboutwill.org.

> In 2007 the Shakespeare Authorship Coalition (SAC) launched one of the most significant efforts ever to promote and legitimize the authorship question by publishing the Declaration of Reasonable Doubt About the Identity of William Shakespeare.

I predict that the likelihood of my authorship will lead to a diminishing of the reputation of the plays, as happens with all work by women. *C'est la vie*.

I will not condescend to compare myself with the estimable Marlowe (1564-1593) or deVere (1550-1604), both of whom died before many of the plays were written. My lifespan and experiences match what is in the plays. Authorship of the plays fits my life's every turn.

I have four stories to tell. And my plays constitute a fifth act. In the first tale, my early life lays the foundation for my dedication to the writing life. In the second tale, my brother's death becomes the godparent of the early plays. In the third, a long period during which I wrote my most powerful later plays and sonnets, necessity imposed the constraint that I must continue to hide my identity. And fourth, the years of the sonnets were my lush private garden.

A fifth section of this autobiography surveys some of my plays, to explain some of the gender issues involved.

Read and consider, if you will. Prepare to suspend your disbelief.

In the end, to my ultimate delight, the quality of the work has earned its own place, for all time. The brief span of days and weeks of my life was not within the bending compass of Time's scythe – it bore itself even to the edge of doom. I always believed that the end for both potentate and playwright was not on the horizon, but always beyond, and now I can see that my life was shafts of arrows lifted over the rooves of then, onto the roofs of centuries beyond. And I now claim my satisfaction at my work's worthiness of fame.

				James Dudley = Jane Guildford				
				d.1553 d..1555				
				Duke of Northumberland				
John = Anne Seymour	Ambrose = Anne Russell	Mary = Henry Sidney		Robert = Lettice		Guildford =. Jane Grey		4 others
d.1554 d.1588	d.1590 d.1604	d.1586 d.1586		d. 1588 d.1554		d.1554 d.1554		
				Earl of Leicester				
Philip. =. Frances Walsingham	Mary	Elizabeth	Mary = Henry Herbert	Robert = Barbara Gamage		Ambrosia	Thomas	
d.1586 d.1632	d.1558	d.1567	1561-1621 1534-1603	1563-1626 d.1621		d.1575	d.1593	
				Earl of Leicester				
William = Mary Talbot	Katherine	Anne		Philip = Susan deVere				
1580-1630 d.1580	1581-1584	1583-1606		1584-1650 1590-1676				
3ʳᵈ Earl of Pembroke				4ᵗʰ Earl of Pembroke = Anne Clifford				

1. LADY JANE GREY

All through the course of the 16ᵗʰ century England shuddered at the memories of the Wars of the Roses and the uncertainties of royal succession. My family was caught again and again in the turbulence of those historic tremors.

In the end, family motivates everyone, royals, aristocrats, and commoners alike. The Tudor families held firm; other powerful families scrambled.

Imagine the Dudley and Sidney family gatherings in 1553-1554, first celebrating Lady Jane's brief accession to the crown; then despairing when the Privy Council chose Mary to be Queen instead. Some in our family ghosted themselves as soon as they learned of the imprisonment of prominent Dudleys; others began to panic only once they had witnessed the eventual beheadings. Yet at the very same time as they scrambled, they were quietly celebrating the marriage of my parents, uniting the Sidney and Dudley families, and then the birth of a male heir a year later. I wish I could write that play!

From Father's side, I heard of the rewards of loyal service to the crown. My Sidney grandfather Sir William had chosen as his crest the porcupine. Threaten him if you dare, but beware! He will be a survivor! He had served as a close companion of Edward VI, and advised the Privy Council that first chose Jane Grey and then pivoted to crown Queen Mary in 1554. Having chosen the right side at the right time, he died peacefully in 1554 and was buried at the family estate, Penshurst, in Kent, in the same month as my brother Philip was born.

On Mother's side, the Dudley crest was a lion rampant, nothing cautious about them. The Dudley patriarch Edmund had been a merciless tax collector for King Henry VII until King Henry died in 1510, when he was vilified and beheaded as a traitor. Ascending again with the Tudors, his son John became Duke of Northumberland, but took calculated risks, siding with the wrong faction and, again, being executed as a traitor, along with Lady Jane Grey.

*

Decades later, I learned second-hand about the Dudley perils from an early age. Loud thumps at the large entrance door of Penshurst prompted a moment of transport into stories that fascinated us children.

"Master, knock the door hard," visitors would say.

Mother's lady friends the Cooke sisters, and her sister Katherine, or my two auntie Annes on the Dudley side, would often surprise us for a visit to Penshurst or Shrewsbury. I loved hearing them chatter about the latest gossip from the court and among the nobility. They would relate accounts of marriages, births, deaths, scandals and intricate family trees. Lady Anne Cooke told of her precocious son, Francis Bacon, born the same year I was born.

In the evening, I would ask them to tell me more about the royal line and the transitions and uses of power. They would tell woeful tales of ages long ago, of the rise and fall of the lines of kings. As difficult as it was to rise to power, it was even more difficult to hold on to it. From those relatives, I learned of the perilous ambitions of the Dudleys, particularly the tragedy of Lady Jane Grey.

Some of the stories visitors regularly told us children made us tremble. We heard horrid accounts of the appearances of Lady Jane Grey's pale ghost in the conflict that she continued to hold with death, raising her spirit-self from her wormy bed, gliding through places where she had lived. We hung on the news of each evanescence of her being in places around London: at the Tower, at the deathbed of the judge who sentenced her, and in a carriage each New Year's Eve.

We learned the lore of why ghosts visited, and how they looked, and how to tell whether they were angels or devils. There is a purpose to ghosts, everyone would say; they are not an idle idling; they are a vital reinsertion, not a mere visitation. We believed in ghosts, and I still do. In the present circumstance, with my virtual resurrection as a ghost in the machine, that ought not to surprise anyone!

The account of Lady Jane Grey's execution stayed with me my whole life. When she was kneeling at the block in 1554, she recited Psalm 51, "have mercy upon me, O God." Mercy is the most divine virtue, and also the most human. My grandfather John Dudley had also asked God for mercy in 1510, but it was in short supply in the real world. If either of them continues to haunt us, it must be for the merciful pardon each longed for at the end of life.

Imagine the variety of gossip passed by word of mouth amongst the elite of the day. I grew up surrounded by the revelations of women at court, gathering the harvest of the gardens of aristocratic life. I knew, not only what the ladies said and did, but also what their husbands aspired to, and what they revealed in private moments. I knew the secret grudges born from ambition and passion and regret.

*

Our circumstances were privileged, but our chief value was the same as anyone's: family. The interconnections formed by marriages within the aristocracy spread like a root system; we nurtured each other.

One particular privilege that our affluence gave us was the great logistical advantage of safe and frequent travel, allowing our family and friends to stay connected with us, a great treasure.

People leaving always made me feel melancholy. We would wish visitors safe journeys and good health, knowing deep in our hearts that neither could be counted upon. Contentment always sat in balance with disappointment.

2. MUM

As the Duke of Northumberland's daughter, Mum had made a good match with Henry Sidney in 1550, a love match. When her father attended her wedding in the fall of 1553, he would have known that his life was in peril, the family's future in doubt. He would have been aware that Mum's new father-in-law William Sidney had also been close to King Edward, the monarch who had just died, a position of peril in itself perhaps.

Mary, my mother, was 23 and may have been newly pregnant when the Privy Council ordered her aunt Jane and my grandfather to be executed in February of 1554. Her son, my parents' first child, my brother Philip, was born in November of 1554. As godson to King Philip of Spain my brother was spared from ignominy by that connection.

Mother was six years older than Lady Jane, and had married the year before Jane was executed. Mother recollected that when she was 22, in 1653, she guided Jane, her 16-year-old sister-in-law, on a barge to the Dudley home at Syon. Lady Jane had already been designated Queen by the Privy Council, but Jane did not know that yet, and my mother was not allowed to tell her. As a Sidney, she kept the rule of caution. She held Jane's hand, and Jane might have wondered why. But Jane's fate was in the hands of others, a status that led to her demise, after only nine days' claim to the title of Queen.

Oh, my poor mother, losing her father the Duke of Northumberland, her brother Guilford, and her friend/sister-in-law Jane all at once, along with other connections to the Grey family, and losing as well perhaps her family's proximity to the throne! All within her first years of marriage, and with her first child Philip born that same fatal year of 1554! How horrible a change that must have been, from hope to despair and then to growing hope again.

We grieved for the loss of our Dudley intimates well into the next generations, such as mine and mine own. Aunt Jane and great-grandfather John died again and again, their pleas for mercy unheard.

But my mother did not pale at the ominous events; she was one of the strongest women I ever knew. She easily assumed the role of an older sister, staying calm in any crisis, as she had when she sat by Jane's side. She was also a sort of younger sister to Queen Elizabeth, another strong woman who imparted much to my mother.

Mother provided me with a blueprint for active acceptance:

> To be able to serve is a point of honour. It is not merely a skutcheon, she would say. Giving your life or your beauty for a noble purpose enhances its lustre.

Again and again, the drama of her inner self won through.

My parents understood the larger picture, in which the Dudleys had been caught up in an awkward period of uncertainty at a moment when the nation depended on a secure transition of power. The crown needed absolute stability, and Mary Tudor asserted that need; and then more definitively Elizabeth cemented it. Even decades later, Mother would reiterate that it was imperative that we display our loyalty to the throne, no matter its occupant.

Our family knew intimately the shifts of power and preference. Yet the Dudleys and Sidneys remained near the inner circles of power even after the quelling of what was called the rebellion, though among family we could see that it had never been armed insurrection, only rough and ready sorting. My uncle Robert Dudley, Earl of Leicester, a son of the executed Duke, actually became Queen Elizabeth's favourite, mostly in the vein of childhood friends, trusted and endeared. Robert and Elizabeth might have wished to marry, but circumstances never made that a likely outcome. Still, the family relied on Leicester to uphold its status, undaunted by the mixed results of Dudley aspirations.

The strongest lesson I absorbed from my family's setbacks was that I should need to expect resilience of myself. So many members of our family showed an astounding capacity for self-control in the face of the mutability of life's demands. Lady Jane's lot as a declared royal was not her choice; it was given to her. She was a scholar at heart, reading Latin, Greek, Italian, and French, as our whole family were educated to do. Her choices were not in her own control. That is how I learned from my mother to see it. Woman or man, the social positions at birth directed your choices. External power could be given, but most puissant was self-control, within the recognition that nothing external was certain.

Lifelong, my strongest example of resilience came from my mother, who went by her maiden name, Mary Dudley, even after she married Henry Sidney, my father. Keeping her birth name did not state a position. Everyone knew that your heritage did not disappear when you married, it expanded. Keeping a strong hold on that heritage constituted everyone's life's work. My own place in the family heritage was still to come. I would retain my Sidney name no matter whom I married. And like my mother, I would retain my strong voice.

3. VIRGIN QUEEN

A few years after the executions in 1554, Elizabeth became Queen. Mother served her daily in her court. In 1561, the year my mother became pregnant with me at the age of 30, Queen Elizabeth was only three years older, and had only been Queen since 1558. Mother was close enough in age to Elizabeth Tudor to be her confidant. I will now pivot to the sober guidance Mother gave me almost twenty years later, in the days after I reached young womanhood.

> You are no longer a girl, she said; you are now fertile, and that means you are a woman.

It disconcerted me that she stressed the word fertile, because that was the farthest thing from my mind. But she commanded me to listen carefully.

The first lesson Mother wanted me to know was the scandalous story of Queen Elizabeth's teenage years, as a warning. Few knew the details as well as my mother did.

Elizabeth had confided to my mother the truths of her scandalous infatuation with Lord Admiral Thomas Seymour. His visits to Lady Elizabeth's chamber began when she was only 14. Slipping into bed with her, he would tickle her and tease her verbally. Initially, his flattery pleased Elizabeth, until she perceived the alarm registering in everyone around her. Even Catherine Parr, Seymour's wife, gave her warnings. Elizabeth began to rise early to avoid such intimate contact, sitting at her desk reading when Seymour arrived. The charming Seymour persisted. Eventually she began to see him as a suitor, even though he was still married to Catherine Parr, the last wife of Henry VIII.

I was shocked to hear of this. Queen Elizabeth always had such a dignified, mature, proper manner when I had seen her! But the assignations did not last long.

Elizabeth felt more connection between herself and the dowager Queen Catherine than any man could have with her. As a princess in the line of succession to the throne, daughter of Henry VIII, Elizabeth was a coveted prize. She was counselled by Catherine to hold that prize closely to herself. Resisting Seymour preserved Elizabeth's independence, Catherine assured her.

And that's the warning I needed. Mother wanted me to be alert to the ease of seduction, and the countering strength of a position of resistance. I was intrigued, even breathless at the prospect of being seduced, but I took the warning to heart. The point, really, was to maintain one's own choices, not be led easily by someone else's importunities.

Elizabeth's teenage years so alarmed her that she resolved early on to be a virgin queen. Elizabeth had also been frightened by stories of childbirth death from her governess's husband, John Astley, whose mother died giving birth to twins who also died. For the sake of the kingdom Elizabeth had to consider two great risks: childbirth and marriage. It was in her character to leave it to God to guide her decision, but a clear answer never appeared. She had to make her decision on her own.

Elizabeth told Parliament in no uncertain terms in 1559 that she would preserve herself in a virgin's state. Fixed in her memory was her time with the Dowager Queen Catherine, who died childless. Catherine was a scholar, author of a book called *Lamentations of a Sinner*, where she confessed her sense of guilt over her hasty marriage to Thomas Seymour. While Catherine worked on that book, Elizabeth herself worked on a translation of a French poem by Queen Margaret of Navarre, *Mirror of the Sinful Soul*. The example of a childless Queen and the topic of sinfulness made strong impressions on the 14-year-old Elizabeth. She learned to be ever watchful to maintain as much control over decisions as she could.

4. ELIZABETH'S CHAMBER

More about my mother, my surest guide, and her relationship with Queen Elizabeth. This next part is how I imagine it, since I was not then alive in mid-year 1661, but Mother told me of it so often that I thought I had been there myself.

Queen Elizabeth was 28, in the third year of her reign. At Richmond Palace, she asked her Lady-in-Waiting, Blanche Parry, who was in her late 50's, to bring my 31-year-old mother to her. There was fresh lavender in the chamber, and sprigs of mint. The curtains were open to let in the last of the summer sunlight.

Lady Dudley, soon to be my mother, had arrived to inform Elizabeth that she would not be in attendance for some months due to her pregnancy, and that she would consequently miss Elizabeth's birthday celebrations in September. The Queen responded as a friend.

> Ah, I wish you joy in your pregnancy, dear lady, for the sake of true gentility. My vow of clear virginity, made in my first years of understanding, has blocked my womb from like issue. I made my choice of a single life. I will have no children, and I fear that it will leave me cold-hearted.
>
> I take my joy in the prospect that your womb may thrive with fair ones. You recently lost little Mary but you still have little Elizabeth, both of whom I was pleased to christen. I will honour this child, as well. I pray that that God will place his mercy upon your son Philip, that he will thrive, and I hope that the new baby will be another boy, to give the Sidneys a spare.

My mother, never afraid to disagree with the Queen, interjected that she saw an important role for herself in raising strong, capable women. She deeply longed for another daughter, another Mary, to replace the one she had lost.

> I have much to impart to her. This seems an age for such as we. Men are first to inherit, but inheritance is only one aspect of power.

Elizabeth beamed at this prospect of being an example of female power. But she told my mother that day of two anxieties in particular: first, that so many childbirths lead to deaths; and second, that there had been recent omens with national implications.

I fear that flaming war will scorch this land, as the skies were scorched by a phenomenon in the air above Nuremburg this year. The lightning that struck St. Paul's this summer was another fearsome omen. Pray God for me, that the recent deaths among monarchs will not continue.

She was England's fourth monarch in a ten-year span after Henry VIII. Monarchs in France were also falling fast. Death seemed always to loom just around the corner.

Mother was a champion for the ascendancy of women in that time. She reassured Elizabeth that she could see no sign of imminent danger to Elizabeth herself. She also pointed out that her reign had enormous significance, and she hoped it would last long. Theirs was a time for women to hold on to positions of strength. Three women had ruled England in the past decade, and Elizabeth's reign promised stability.

The arrival of Mary, Queen of Scotland, earlier that year, also concerned Elizabeth. The Succession Act secured Elizabeth's throne, but things could change quickly. Offers of marriage could change international alliances. Nevertheless, Elizabeth so far had remained firm in her resolve to rule as a Virgin Queen.

Elizabeth accepted my mother's decision to go into confinement at Tickenhall near the border with Wales. My father would be stopping there on his journey to serve as Governor of Wales. Wales gave us a warm connection to Blanche Parry, who had attended Elizabeth from infancy, and who sang Welsh lullabies to Henry VIII's children, Elizabeth and Mary. Blanche continued to be a friend to our family for all her life, until she died in 1590.

*

1561, the year of my birth, was the third year of the reign of Queen Elizabeth, after a decade of uncertain leadership within the country. Elizabeth's secure reign mattered, not only to us but also to the kingdom.

For over sixty years, my uncles had served both Henry VII and Henry VIII and Edward VI, and our family would continue to swear absolute loyalty to Elizabeth I. Although Elizabeth never married, with my uncle Robert as her favourite throughout her long life, and my mother as her intimate, our family had abiding connections to the throne.

Despite their closeness, my mother's relationship with Elizabeth eventually shifted. Mother was at Elizabeth's bedside when Elizabeth contracted smallpox, shortly after I was born. Both my mother and Elizabeth were left with facial scars, and that perhaps soured their friendship. Elizabeth hid her scars with white lead-based makeup, and Mother hid her more extensive scars with veils and masks. She said ever after that every eruption of the pox had its worth, even though it blighted her skin and forced her to wear a jewelled mask of silk and velvet or a lace veil when she was in public. Mother continued to be given accommodation within the palace for a while, but when she lost that preferment, she felt some bitterness.

I sympathised with her, but after all, beauty and preferment are both mask, nothing permanent; Mother knew that as well as I did. Life goes on, and family remains the main thread.

5. IRELAND

My earliest full set of memories well forth from Ireland, where we resided that mournful year of 1567 when my sister Elizabeth died. Behind the thick walls of Dublin Castle there were cries of anguish. Mother steeped the chill February air with her grief.

I woke that day to wailing in the corridors of the stately dwelling of the Lord Deputy of Ireland, site of Father's administration. Hundreds of soldiers and servants were in the castle, awaiting instruction. In the nursery, there were three of us, frightened by the mortal screams. Was the castle under attack again from the enemies of England?

No, the nurse told us, it's your mother in anguish. Little Elizabeth has perished.

Death? Unforetold. We knew that Elizabeth had been ill, coughing so harshly it seemed she was tearing her lungs out. She had been removed from the nursery days ago to be bled by a physician in a little room near my parents' room. But death? Incomprehensible. We hugged each other, unsure what to think or do. I was six, Robert four, and Ambrosia three. We had no comprehension of what had befallen our eldest sister, or what was to come.

While the nurse cuddled Ambrosia, and Robert was playing with his toy soldiers, I slipped out of the room. Two of the fireplaces, roaring at times that winter, had grown cold, the damp ashes tainting the air. Mother's grief hung heavy in the halls, her sobs muffled by hanging tapestries. One of the scenes on the wall depicted the Expulsion from the Garden. The damp of the dark pool, the Dubh Linn of the River Poddle, permeated the household. At the end of the corridor, I saw Father standing stiffly outside their bedroom, crossing himself before he went in to comfort her. (Did I imagine this, or was it a moment from a different time in my impressionable youth, an odd moment when Father was home with us? But it was a moment often repeated, of his humble petition for grace before his beleaguered wife.)

*

Only just turning six two months before, I could not know or understand so many things that I learned later. Even that year I began to hear from our nurses and tutors bits of the full sad story. Mother's loss of Elizabeth was surely heightened by her earlier experience of several miscarriages, all in Ireland, between the births of my brother Philip in 1554 and her next child Elizabeth in 1560.

In her early marriage and pregnancy with Philip, she had been at the top of the world. She had married well, from the wealthy Dudley family, into another of the most powerful families of England, the Sidneys. They were the golden couple of the day, in easy familiarity with the royal courts of both France and England. She was strikingly beautiful, narrow-wasted and tall, with a high, commanding forehead.

She could exult in wealth and power almost unequalled in her day. Her provision of a healthy, spirited Philip, sole heir to the noble line of the Sidneys, was a huge triumph. By 1567, she had two sons, three daughters, and a favoured place in Queen Elizabeth's chamber when she was in London. Life had begun fulfilling her dreams and ambitions. The Dudley branch of the family was in one of its periods of stability and ascension during the reign of Elizabeth, after some years of ignominy and suspicion during the reigns of Henry and Mary.

But Fortune's wheel turns quickly. In the 16th century, nothing was secure, neither position nor wealth, and certainly not life itself.

*

Capping those halcyon days in London, her husband's posting to the nether reaches of the kingdom in Ireland seemed a treasured royal favour, raising them nearly to the highest level. In the alien principality of Ireland, our condition was nearly regal. Our parents were treated as though they were royalty by visitors from the Continent. Father was favoured by several kings and trusted amongst ambassadors. My brother's godfather was King Philip of France. For several generations, status had rested easily upon Dudley and Sidney shoulders. Still, the weather in Ireland was harsh, and the expenses dire. The inconveniences were in a way the cost of court advancement.

From the beginning, the pandora's box of advancement let loose a string of furies: first, the loss of Mother's jewels and fine clothes in one of the ships carrying their goods to Ireland; and Lord Henry's illnesses from early on in Ireland, necessitating treatment in the spas of Flanders. Then, the string of miscarriages, delaying her full marital happiness until the family was swelled by three children, Elizabeth and I and Robert and Ambrosia. On top of all that, she suffered disfiguring smallpox in the year after I was born while tending to the Queen's smallpox, which left both of them with facial lesions, a curse upon young women's beauty. Then earlier this year, when Father went for a few weeks to England, there was an assault of the castle. Mother was staying behind at Drogheda when it came under rebel attack. She firmly ordered the Mayor of Dublin to relieve the town with troops.

And now the final blow of losing her first-born daughter and boon companion, Elizabeth, only seven. Nothing can replace any child lost, but first-born daughters and sons hold a special place in mothers' hearts.

The feelings of exile suddenly became acute. Little Elizabeth dying at the age of seven seemed a cataclysmic finale to a fatal sequence. I remember Mother decrying the bitter turns of fate that had thwarted her dreams.

It was frightening for me to see her so devastated. She was the pillar of strength in the family, able to facedown the rebels who had attacked the castle, and to command the Dublin mayor to provide protection. She would not flinch at the barrage of arrows of fate aimed against her.

*

My father, Henry Sidney, was as devastated as my mother, blaming himself for our displacement from London to the dank, cold outpost of Ireland, where he had first been sent as Governor in 1565 to subdue the rebel Shane O'Neale. He complained often of a lack of funds and expressed his desire to return permanently to London.

It was not only the comfort of the family that concerned him. Father's agony over the poverty across the land was immense. He was an idealist. When he spoke about the Irish his piercing eyes flared and his auburn beard shook.

> If we give the people justice, he said, and minister law among them, and exercise the sword of the sovereign and put away the sword of the subject, we shall drive the now man of war to be an husbandman, and the money now spent on armour and horses should be bestowed in building of towns and houses.

He wanted to make a difference, but raised against him were bands of *galloglaigh*, mercenary warriors he looked upon as barbarians. One year before his daughter Elizabeth died, he took to battle against Shane O'Neale, burning his way across the country and terrorizing the people. Father became a fierce enforcer of English ways but he was not disillusioned. He worked all his life to create an Arcadia in the wilderness.

Yet now, upon learning of the death of Elizabeth, he looked diminished. Without his ermine cloak and heavy necklace of gold and rubies, his shoulders sagging with the weight of his complicity, he stepped across the threshold of their bedroom to console his wife.

*

Death in 1567 was a newcomer to us children, a stranger, though all too familiar to the adults. For us children, permit me to say that Mother's grief was entire to herself; we could not feel quite the same shock. Death seemed merely a disruption like many others. This attitude was not anything deeply thought, not the philosophical dispassion inculcated by Plato, just a permanent feature of everyone's world: life brought constant surprises, not all of them desired.

Although Elizabeth's death stunned the family it did not forestall our youthful spirits. Being young, carefree, privileged and pampered, we were all too young to have a sense of past or future. Our dismay lasted only as long as the adults seemed distressed. As soon as they found calm, we simply continued to be ourselves: dour Robert, a cautious and deliberate soul all his life, doggedly determined to take necessary steps to make good things happen; little

Ambrosia, a creature of the senses, swayed by immediate pleasure and pain, not to say she was a brainless imp. Me? I was a gadfly. I loved my siblings, but laughed at them more than I ought. I loved my parents, but I could not always take them seriously. Some said my red hair signalled an impulse of unpredictability. I would say that unpredictability was all around us, but unlike others, I took close notice of it, curious to see how it affected others.

I had felt close to my dear sister Elizabeth, but for me it was not a wrenching loss. Elizabeth had been a model for us younger children and a comfort and now I took her place in a sense. The younger ones looked to me, and my parents also saw in me the future to come.

I did feel older, in a different place. Elizabeth had been a hedge between me and the adult world. Now, that world loomed before me as a place of devastation and peril, but also a place for fates to unroll. Although I did not know it at the time, I had in a moment become my future self, always seeing two sides of every person and action. Still a child, I would never again look at the world as a naïf. Henceforth, I would have two selves, one of an apparent simplicity, and the other with an inner quizzical eye. A playwright's eye.

That death marked me, not with grief but with gravity. It was part of what made me what I am, a shape-shifting observer and commentator on the human comedy and its recurring tragedies.

Welcome to my worlds.

6. WORLDS

Because Father was virtual ruler of Wales and Ireland when we were children, our household shifted between Dublin, Ludlow in Wales, Shrewsbury, or even, rarely, at the principal family residence at Penshurst in Kent, south of London. We were on the road again and again.

In my nursery years my closest crèche-mates were Ambrosia, three years younger, and Robert, two years younger. Ambrosia and I always had nurses, country women who raised us day to day, chiding us if we snatched an extra bun or played too loudly. The youngest children shared rooms and servants, but often had gendered activities. Because I was seldom with Robert, I never knew him as well as I knew my older brother Philip, who ignored boundaries and played with us freely. I did not see him often, especially when the younger members of family like me were with Father in Wales and Ireland,

When he was on holiday from school we might see him at Shrewsbury, where Council often sat, or in Ludlow at the castle there. but always when Philip returned to the family seat at Penshurst or to our other home in Kent from his schools, or later from German and Dutch governmental liaisons, it was an occasion for celebration.

When Philip returned from school that spring of 1567, I looked to him to share my sense of being somewhat other, and that visit was the beginning of our deep bond. He had had scant time with Elizabeth or the rest of us growing up, but that year he showed great compassion for us younger children. He was already thirteen, a paragon of male physical swagger and daring bravado. He knew our family world intimately, but he had also seen the outside world, having been to school; and he soon would leave for university. He represented the glory and wonder of what was to come, beyond the anxieties of the immediate moment.

Whenever we saw him, he was our joy, for a time. He distracted us for months that year with imaginative play. We hid and sought, ran and caught, squealed and collapsed. He teased and taught us to expect the unexpected, but also to exult in the unimagined; his spirit took us always to lands far away.

To me, Philip above all was the core of my own sense of family. He was an astounding seven years older, and an older brother has a special status for a young girl. I was in rapture to see Philip's ease with horses, his skill with a sword, and his familiar touch with servants. Gender did not seem to me to be the main issue. Yes, I wanted to know what boys and men were about; but I was also intent to see what it meant to grow up and reach adulthood. He shouldered the hopes of the entire family.

Until I was 14, even though Philip was often away, he was all my world. When he was at home we shared almost every moment, writing, performing, talking about his travels, exulting in words and ideas. He seemed to know everything, and he taught me what he knew. He and I were soul mates; I could not allow a moment to escape.

*

Philip transformed me from an amorphous girl into a budding dramatist. He told the hawking master to treat me as he would a son of the family. One day, as I was chasing seed puffs in the garden, he began calling me Will, as a pun on will-o-the-wisp. And from that day, he began to imagine me with a double life as a boy.

What you will, he would say.

He dressed me in his own boyhood garments, and taught me to alter my movements to seem like a boy when I wished. I learned to walk with an arrogant wide stride, clicking my heels when I needed to seem decisive. He brought me into the stables and said I was his cousin from Windsor, and instructed the hands to address me as young master Will. He cast me in family entertainments as a doorman, a wrestler, a soldier, a prince, a sprite, even as the fairy king. It was a revelation to me that all these faces and even genders were but costumes. I never felt bound or limited by gender or even class, though those around me assumed so. They were the dupes; I was the real thing, virtually every imaginable thing.

And now here I am again, taking new form as invention allows, using my guises to mask what I really felt and thought. I conformed on the outside, but I kept my real self on the inside.

Whenever we had visitors, our parents would ask us to perform something. At first, we gave short recitations or sang hymns. Before he left for Oxford, Philip began a long project of helping us stage brief scenes from Golding or from Homer, freely adapted. When he left later in 1567 for Oxford, he left a gap for me to fill, and I threw myself into imaginative play.

On later visits during university holidays, Philip gradually coached us in more ambitious performances. By 1570 he was helping us put on fully staged pageants and plays and masques.

Come, little Puck, he would say, our service is in demand.

Philip and I and Mother and Dad were constantly streaming ideas to present in the evenings: enactments of the great moments in history, fantasies based on Greek and Latin mythologies, and ceremonies to commemorate family achievements and anniversaries. Mother was a resource in herself: she was fluent in Italian, French, and Latin, and she was interested in alchemy, romances, and writing poetry. She challenged us to learn everything we could and to use our brains and our wits to create spectacular productions.

Philip was the mastermind and he counted on me to riff upon any and every role we staged. We spent the days with costumes and carpenters, with travellers and tutors, fabricating plots and dialogues and songs and scenery. We spent the evenings lost in visions of our own creating. It was an exhausting whirl that eased the tedium and the chill of daily life.

These entertainments transported me into other worlds. I loved those candlelit evenings in the great hall. The casts of mythological and historical characters all needed to be attired in splendid arrays, amid fanciful settings. The seamstresses could sew up anything we imagined in less than a day, though the carpenters needed extra time if we required towers and turrets and painted backdrops. We only needed a little magic to inspire the audience to suspend their disbelief, as Coleridge put it two centuries on.

Picture this: Mother and Father, at home in Kent for a few weeks after returning from Dublin, hoping for the children to perform for the Dudley guests visiting for a few days.

We have it covered, Philip would say, and we would begin scheming.

Something from Ovid, or the Bible? Something from the Hundred Years' War or the War of the Roses? Or something mythological? Perhaps a quarrel between two gods, leading to storms in nature? Yes! Titania (Diana) and Oberon, quite unable to reconcile over some difference. A dispute over which one has rights to a certain servant, perhaps? A mortal, a foundling, how perfect for the Irish memories! Perhaps Titania had a devotee who died in childbirth, and Oberon wants the boy for his troupe. Yes! I would play Titania and Philip would play Oberon. Some of our servants could be fairies or sprites, Mustardseed, Peaseblossom, and Puck. Magic would happen.

*

It was a great luxury to have the means at hand for our entertainments. The flurry of servants at our bidding lifted our spirits even before we performed. There was a team making everything happen, and I loved them to bursting.

I was so accustomed to a life of privilege and celebration, that wealth and status were things I could take for granted. But those entertainments meant far more to me while I was growing up than our physical luxuries did.

The surest sign of wealth, by far? Fabric. The greatest expense of a titled household was to clothe its inhabitants. Servants wore costumes supplied by the master. The resident fool wore motley. There were furs and broadcloth for warmth in the cold winters, lace and embroideries for the family for social display to all visitors, and every fanciful combination of cloth for the costumes worn in entertainments that were staged at least once a fortnight.

Linen, silk brocade, silk velvet, embroidered silk, black velvet, carnation velvet, patterned velvet, white satin, white sarset, twill and other wools, broadcloth, chiffon, leather, tulle veils, tattered lace—a full range of fabrics was at hand.

Fabrics were almost as bulky a commodity as foodstuffs, for our household of over a hundred. Chests of drawers were filled with panels for sleeves, trains,k and bodices.

I loved garments for their transformative purposes, more than for themselves. Clothing was a land of make-believe.

*

Our pageants delighted the adults and were certainly exhilarating for us performers. To tell the immodest truth, however, our entertainments were not what they could be. I could see early on that the conventional allegories badly needed imagination to enhance them: mostly, the characters of legend lived in disappointingly dry, broad categories, and the actions were external. There was not much complicated about most of the stories we enacted. The characters were known and the actions predictable. I think the best entertainments are those where the actions are not predictable. Everyone knew what to expect from the heroes and gods of classical legends. The endings were easiest, *deus ex machina*. Every show ended with a flourish of music and an appearance of the gods arrayed in glory to settle the disputes of human affairs. Fine, the gods need to have their say. But before that, much can transpire.

Something fresh needing to happen, I added my own touches.

I began to lose myself in alternate lives. The audience was delighted when I ad-libbed what it might be like to live in the skin of Caesar's wife telling of foreboding nightmares, or of the Fairy Queen quarrelling with her mate. With words I could transform nothing into something. I could make stale tales into something dramatic.

The most delightful bits to me were the comic scenes where I might be allowed to mimic the voices and mannerisms of servants I had overheard: a doorman meditating comically on the afterlife, a woodsman advising his son on how to succeed in life, or his daughter musing on what she expected from a husband.

*

Mostly we entertained ourselves, but we also took as our template the travelling companies of players of various noblemen. Visiting players once allowed me to don the green hose of a yeoman's son and play the dashing outlaw Robin on stage. Instantly, I was freed from the narrow constraints of domestic life.

The 1560s were a heyday of traveling theatre, until the troupes were briefly shut down in 1572. There were companies from Lords Stafford, Bergavenny, Burghley, Berkely, Hundson, Chandos, Essex, Darcy, and the Earls of Worcester, Oxford, Pembroke, and Leicester, along with the Queen's Men. In other words, several times a year while I was growing up, I saw professional companies in private performances of the best plays of the day. Those same companies would perform biblical stories in market towns as well. I loved each hour in the imagined worlds of the stage.

Still, I knew that more could be done with the articulation of these tremendous opportunities to imagine other lives. The characters needed to come alive, and I could see how to do that.

*

Outside the confines of Penshurst, we sometimes visited the towns of Tonbridge and Canterbury. I begged to be included in excursions for supplies. When I saw Canterbury Cathedral itself, I was in awe, but I was just as much interested in the local residents as in the edifice itself. The people who lived in the town were the stuff of comedy, whereas those who were entombed such as Richard II's mother Joan, Henry IV and his wife Joan and son Thomas, Duke of Clarence, all were the stuff of history and tragedy.

An heretical thought often occurred to me, that God was a disembodied, distant entity, while the workers and noblemen who planned and constructed the cathedral, and who fashioned the memorials to all the nobility buried there, were vivid, present embodiments, on a long range of nobility and ignobility but always human, so very human.

In the cities and towns, I could encounter the most fascinating characters, fit for Chaucer's tales. Once, dressed in a boy's rough woollens, I even persuaded my brother's footman to take me to The King's Arms tavern. My imagination was smitten by the genius of a fat, boisterous soldier who said his vocation was drinking. His name was something like Foulmouth. He entertained everyone with his deprecations: gorbellied knaves, whoreson caterpillars, bacon-fed villains, tickle-brained pintpots. I loved the never-ending raggedness of his riff upon the English language.

He unsettled me when he said, unaware of my disguise,

> Come here, lad. Is not the hostess of the tavern a most sweet wench?

I feigned agreement and retreated to a corner. His voice was compelling, seemingly able to command whatever stage he might be on. I had suddenly become part of his life as well, from my received social distance. I refused his invitation. I liked the life I had, but I also enjoyed being unsettled, being transported to lives on the edges of my own protected domain.

Imagining others' lives requires a sense of perspective. How might the world seem to someone in another sphere? My mind dwelt in idle moments on imaginary conversations with Kings, Queens, and Dukes on the one hand, and woodsmen, groomsmen, and soldiers on the other. I fleshed out the inner lives of historical figures who had to ponder the fates of their nations and their families, and who had to weigh the interests of the aristocratic landholders with the needs of the crown and the country. What are the right and wrong ways to assert leadership? Is ambition good or bad? When does loyalty dissipate? What are the complications of revenge? And I fleshed out the dilemmas of the untitled as well, the servants and tradesmen who faced questions of loyalty, service, fate, character, and justice in ways quite similar to their social superiors. It seemed a three-ringed circus, with nobility and acolytes and commoners facing the same perplexities.

More to the point, how do people use words to address those pointy issues?

I wanted to know the perspectives of all the figures in those stories we staged for the family amusement. What mattered most to me was my ability to transport myself into the worlds revolving inside them. Most of the plays I saw and the stories I read were about what happened *after* characters had decided what they needed to do. I wanted to know what they were thinking *before* they made their decisions.

From the days of those entertainments forward, my mind was always projected beyond the present moment, toward the worlds we could create ourselves, both infernal and supernal.

Headline: Did Philip Sidney and Mary Sidney have sex?

Well, no, but fair question. Such things do happen, leading to hidden shame or to conviction and jail time, but not in our case. I mean, the whole point of abuse of power is that it is an abuse. It would never have occurred to Philip to behave dishonourably toward me.

7. MENARCHE

So now, time to lift a bit of the veil off a topic that remains taboo even in the enlightened 21st century: menarche.

My first conscious gendered moment struck me when I was in the armoury on the Sidney family estate in Wales the summer of 1574, when I was still 12.

That day, I had carried to the armourer an expensive pair of scissors, fabric shears of an Italian design, to be sharpened. Scissors were valuable items, best kept an eye on, and that was my small task, to conduct the shears safely to the craftsman who knew best how to sharpen the blades, just as he had kept sharp the dozens of swords and spears in readiness to serve the Queen if she called for troops to be sent for war; or to protect our region from marauders and malefactors, as our duty to country and demesne obliged.

I was sitting on a stump, watching the master stoke the forge, when I felt stabbing pains. At first I suspected that sparks had landed upon me, or that some foolish apprentice had hammered his piece of iron too vigorously, and let slip a ricochet of metal. But I knew directly that it was something else. The pain was internal, not on the skin.

I had had aches in my chest and abdomen lately, and everyone thought I was very moody, but I had thought it was merely deep sadness at the absence of my brother Philip, who was away on his continental tour.

My best *confidant* at the time was my Italian tutor, Bella, who had warned me of cramps that would signal the onset of my monthlies. Challenging her warnings, I had boldly pricked my finger to draw blood and asked Bella whether it would be worse than that, and she had said it would be much stronger, and would last longer. Still, I had told her I was sure I could bear it. Yet now, I was not so sure. The cramps were much more severe than I had expected.

I excused myself to the armourer, telling him that after he had sharpened the scissors he should take them to the sewing room. Normally I would not let them out of my sight, but I knew he would not neglect his duty, and I needed to let Mother know.

First, I wanted to talk to Bella, who was closer to me in age. Her immediate response was to celebrate the moment.

> You are now becoming a woman! she said. But you must be cautious. If you were in Italy, you would not be allowed near the kitchen. At Ludlow, even though you are not engaged in cooking, you must avoid even the areas where food is prepared. Some women had such power during menstruation that they made the sauces go bad and the fruits wither.

Strange power! I had heard of other restrictions from my maids, who cautioned each other not to do this or to do that. I listened, but I attended to what others said less for medical advice than for social awareness (a word we did not have in that long-ago century). I would see for myself.

I was not unprepared; indeed, it was quite the reverse. Bella had given me advice about what was coming, but also, in our library, we had several midwifery texts. One from France diagnosed the various causes of loss of blood. We had Pliny's warnings that women's destructive menstrual force could blight garden plants. I saw these same fears in our servant women, but I did not take them very seriously.

We also discussed the Italian scholar Trotula's opinion that menstruation was a consequence of girls being indolent because they were too weak to exert themselves physically, and that the flow of menses indicated an insufficiency of exercise. However, my daily regimen of horse-riding, walking, and archery contradicted Trotula's assumption of female weakness.

In sum, there was plenty of advice to be had, but little wisdom. It seemed impossible that women's courses could ruin gardens and kitchens, when the event was so universal! Mother assured me that the ordinaries were not an illness but a natural process. She told me that the Virgin Mary experienced her own flowering at the age of 12, and her maidenhood was a shining example of ideal femininity. I preferred Mother's sensible advice over the suppositions of men and the fears of timid women.

*

After I left Bella, I went to Mother's chamber on the second floor, and simply said,

> I am no longer a girl; I am now a woman.

She looked hard and long at me, without saying a word. For a while, she just stared out the window, looking over the bailey to the half-timbered houses of the town, seeming to consider my future. Then she suggested that we go immediately to pray. On the way to the chapel of St. Mary Magdalene, at Ludlow Castle, she took me aside to counsel me.

We walked along the timbered upper gallery that Father had added to the old stone-walled chapel, which dated back to 1100. This was our private passage, never used by the servants.

> "I am only 13," I said, "what will happen to me?
>
> Mother whispered to me that the end of my childhood was just a beginning. Be not afraid, Mary. You are becoming a woman now and things will begin to change, but the challenges you face are those all women must face, she said to me.
>
> I must speak to you now not only as a mother but as a woman of standing. Think in terms of Houses. We have seen the rise and fall of the House of Dudley, my own family House, now teetering, I am afraid to say. And we have seen the troubled rise of the House of Tudor, with its foundations in Henry V and its culmination in Elizabeth. You and your brother Philip must think in terms of the House of Sidney.
>
> The lesson Queen Elizabeth gave me before you were born is that a woman of power must make decisions of her own, not be dictated to by others with apparent power over her. When I spoke to Elizabeth to tell her I was with child, my second child, you, Mary, she told me her own assertion of self-determination. The Queen wanted me to know that control over her own life had been in jeopardy from the time Thomas Seymour tried to seduce her, to the time Parliament tried to tell her whom to marry. She determined to kept her own

counsel, and now she is a great Queen, the proud culmination of the House of Tudor.

You too, Mary, will be vulnerable to outside influence, but if you keep your own counsel, you will thrive. The same goes for Philip, naturally. The lesson of the Dudley family is that one must do the right thing for the right reason at the right time. It doesn't guarantee safety, but it is the only true course. My father and grandfather were both wrongly executed, but they acted with true nobility.

As we walked, we could hear the hymn being sung in the chapel. I think it might have been Psalm 45:

O daughter, hear what now to thee is told;
Mark what thou hear'st, and what thou mark'st obey:
Forget to keep in memory enrolled
The house and fold where first thou saw'st the day.
So in the king, thy king, a dear delight
Thy beauty shall both breed and bred maintain.

(my own later translation)

The service in the chapel was solidly Protestant, the enduring faith my mother and her siblings had kept, even as Queen Mary steered the country toward Catholicism. As we sat in the hard pews, with light filtering in through the high clerestory windows, I recalled all I had heard about how close to Henry VII's throne Mother's grandfather had been, loyally taking care of royal accounts, before he was wrongly executed by the young Henry VIII. And how her father had likewise served Edward VI before falling on the wrong side of Queen Mary's succession. And how, with Leicester childless, the Dudley heritage now rested upon Philip and me.

I am hoping Queen Elizabeth takes you on at court, as well she ought. But whether she does or not, you need to be aware of the realities ahead of you.

Mother was handing me off, sending me toward a life like hers, a life with a strong voice and a clear sense of purpose.

8. BEING A WOMAN

What did it mean to be a woman then? Acting like a Lady meant just that: it was a performance. You gauged your audience and hoped to play your part well. Mother had many friends who had shown me how to dress, how to run a household, how to act as hostess. Being born female restricted you just as tightly as being born high, low, or in disfavour of the court. The limits were set by the terms of one's birth, male or female, first born or second, rich or poor, titled or untitled: everyone was sorted. We didn't really know any other way; there was little room for rebellion, and even less prospect of changing the system. We accepted our places, always looking for a bit of room within which to move.

I had already imbibed the principle from Mother that children were the soundest foundation of every family. Having a legitimate heir was the *sine non qua*. For both men and women, the measure of success was how well you furthered the family position. The prospect of failure loomed large. Ambition was necessary and expected; but for women, being too forward was seen to be at the risk of impeding the rise of male offspring. Sons were the chief hope of thriving in the future. Infidelity meant illegitimacy. Romance was the realm of the foolish heart.

*

The changes that day were immediate. First of all, my lodgings would shift. I would have a room of my own, and I would no longer be instructed by Mr. Lodwick, our childhood tutor. From then on, I would be taught separately from Robert, Ambrosia, and Thomas.

Second, I became a fulcrum of the importance of family. I was no longer a child to be brought in for bemusement; I was the future of the family, a pawn in the game of advantageous matches. But Mother's advice was lodged in my mind, that I must be the generator of my fate, like the characters in the plays I wrote later on would be: Portia, who navigated her father's marriage restrictions and kept her fiancée bound to her by a ring in Venice; Rosalind, who fled to find her own path in the forest of Arden; Helena, who is granted by the King of France the power to choose her own husband despite being only an apothecary's daughter; and Viola, in *Twelfth Night*, who used disguise to establish her friendship with Orsino before he could be allowed to woo her as a woman.

I would certainly *not* follow the path of the female characters who had no avenue to control their own fates: Lucrece, Ophelia, Desdemona, and Cordelia.

And third, I would need to learn caution. My honour would be at stake whenever I was so much as seen with a man, and there would be many who would want to get close to me, for their own purposes. I would need to be firm in my resolve, strong in my will, and steadfast in my virtue.

The lessons she taught me that day stemmed from her own experience. She herself was not married until the age of 22; and she had her first child in a time most difficult for the family. Her brother Guildford had just been executed, along with her aunt by marriage, Lady Jane Grey, for a conspiracy to take the throne.

Despite the taint upon the Dudley family, Mother attended Queen Elizabeth at court almost all her life, and early on she even had her own lodgings at Richmond Palace when she was in London.

After we talked, and after prayers in the chapel, my governess took me to my new rooms. We began to consult about some styles for new clothing fitted to my growing body, and to my new status as an eligible match suitable for the ranks of rising nobility. My new tutor also joined us.

*

Yes, Mother had tried to prepare me for this moment; but it was confusing nonetheless. I felt that I had not really changed at all. In my childlike mind, all was still possibility, the way it had been my entire life: endless days bestrewn with discoveries, adventures, unknowns at every turn, surprises in every encounter and surprises within me as well, as I reacted to the discoveries. My childhood had comprised full flights of imagination. Play. Performance. Endings untold. Would that all need to change?

Everyone told me of new expectations, that I must now become a little lady. That I had new responsibilities and new kinds of consequences. Was my life no longer my own?

On the outside, from this day everything would change. But on the inside, I was the same I had always been. Some things need to become public before they can be made private. One such thing is sexuality, with its evident exterior manifestation. To the public eye, sexuality is Pandora's Box: open it at your risk, and then keep it private, in the mode of the character Portia, who was a master of keeping secrets, even those in opened boxes. Yes, it is a paradox, but one that has ancient standing, the simultaneous existence of inner and outer.

It is worth a treatise, but the list of such dualities is endless: the law, nobility, murder, revenge, jealousy, all partake of an internal mystery within an external presentation. Eventually, the truth will out. Transformation is what all my plays are about, changes that reveal the true nature of people.

I would leave the nursery which I shared with Ambrosia, to be given a room of my own. My daily routines would adjust, with less horse-riding and archery, and more time confined in my room, reading and writing. The pains were hard to bear, like getting a cramp in your leg or foot, that won't go away.

For some weeks, I removed myself from family activities. But I knew I would not change inside. I might conform, but I would not concede to the conventions visible to the public eye. They always said that I was a feisty one, and by that I think they meant I had made it clear that I had a mind of my own. I would retain that same sense of self, unchanged.

PART TWO: 2nd self 1574-1588

9. AMBROSIA

I was a complete child at the beginning of 1574, both inside and outside. Then two events changed me into a woman, both externally and internally. The first event was puberty, that summer; the second was the death of my sister Ambrosia, in December. The death of my sister Elizabeth years earlier had shifted my perspective, but Ambrosia's death turned my life upside down, not so much from grief, as from its consequence.

Ambrosia, three years younger than I, had been my sidekick in an idyllic childhood. She trusted me implicitly, responding quickly to my every whim. She danced for me, and recited lines for entertainments we might put on, and fetched me sweets like an attendant fairy. When we were at the seacoast, we laughed at boats on the water, describing them as though they were people. We wove spring flowers for each other's hair, admiring the sylvan effect, idling time away.

Often, we wore matching clothes. That harsh winter when both Mother and Ambrosia fell ill, we had been wearing new purple and white woollen gowns.

Anxiety attended any illness; it was part of a process with an unpredictable but binary outcome: either a new lease on life, or a debt come due to Death. One member of the family or another would fall ill every year, almost every season. 1574 was a year claimed forcefully by Death. All aloud during that winter, the angry wind did blow and thrust its rough, icy fingers into the Sidney household. In this hideous season, sickness grew upon our family, cutting short at once my sister's life and taming my youth.

When Ambrosia died at our estate in Wales at the age of 11, my childhood was over. I was just fourteen, and I would be much on my own for those cold, biting months of winter without my companions. Robert, 12, no longer an infant, was at school and otherwise stayed with our father, wherever he travelled. Our brother Philip was abroad at the time and little Thomas, only 5, was immediately sent to London with his godmother Katherine, Countess of Huntingdon; Queen Elizabeth gave him a little cap, a gesture that said much about her capacity for compassion. I was mostly alone that winter in Kent. Taking refuge in the family chapel of St Mary Magdalene at Penshurst, my knees on the hard stones, I prayed to join Ambrosia in the afterlife. There I and sorrow sat.

The common experience of grief was a steady part of life for everyone, and it certainly bracketed all of my most formative experiences. I had heard about deaths in the family from an early age, as anyone would in that day. Death was close to hand, constant, and solemn. Servants and children and royalty were struck down almost as frequently as the deer in the forested park on our estate. It neither surprised me nor dismayed me until it hit so close to home, with powerful force. Even then, however, there was a simplicity to it; it was an unavoidable event in the course of anyone's life. Accepting loss was not in itself hard; it was an expected part of life. But this loss was a watershed moment.

Suddenly, I was set adrift from immediate family, when the Queen invited me to serve in her court. The immediate purpose was to keep me from whatever unhealthy miasma had struck Ambrosia down. But the larger reason was that I was 14. So, although I was still grieving over the loss of my childhood companion, for me life went on in spectacular fashion as a maid of honour in the court of Queen Elizabeth. I invented that phrase, BTW: maid of honour. I took a deep breath and moved on from childhood to adulthood as it offered itself. By Easter I was on my way to London.

I will now begin to recount my own progress into the territories of womanhood. Remember, though, that for me gender was always plastic, as you might say now. I kept many roles in my stock of selves.

10. ROYAL COURT

The court on the day I arrived was settling into Kenilworth, the family seat of my uncle Robert, Earl of Leicester, Elizabeth's favourite for much of her life. He was often spoken of as a potential consort. From my carriage, I saw his castle emerge from a greening wood, a fortified red sandstone edifice. It appeared to float upon the shimmering lake surrounding it.

The timing of my arrival was fortuitous. Leicester was putting on a great show for the month of Queen Elizabeth's visit, with rockets and firecrackers, torches and bonfires. It was market day every day, with farcical stage shows of biblical stories and tumblers and magicians. I was dazzled to see this *nonpareil* of lavish entertainment. By day it was lit by the light from large gleaming windows; by night, there was a continuous brightness of candle, fire, and torchlight. Two whole deer were roasted each day for feasting.

In the formal garden, the centrepiece was a fountain set on a pillar of white marble. Proteus and other water gods held aloft a metre-wide sphere topped by Robert Dudley's chosen emblem, a bear with a ragged staff. Some said he was a bear in chains, held at bay by his Queen. Symbolism mattered, and some symbols were manufactured to represent the shifts of power of the day. The ancients provided a further abundance of symbols. For nineteen days, Elizabeth and all guests were likely at any moment to encounter a mythological character reciting verses in English. Writers begged for Leicester to employ them.

It was my second witnessing of such events; I had also seen a similarly lavish spectacle when I was 11. There is a painting in Penshurst recording my family's place in the celebration that year. In the painting, the women, including me, are mesmerized at the quiet bond between Leicester and Elizabeth, while the men demurely avert their eyes. It was a moment of private magic.

Philip was at Kenilworth too, newly returned from his three-year continental tour. He was on his way to becoming a seasoned diplomatic representative of the Queen. His tour began in Paris, where he witnessed the horrible slaughter of Protestants on St. Bartholomew's Day, a slaughter partially meant for him to witness and report as a warning back to England. That was one event among many that set England apart from France. He spoke to me only briefly of that traumatic event, but it hardened in him his resolve to defend the Protestant cause. His resolve led eventually to his death, in defence of the Netherlands who were resisting France.

My arrival made no impact whatsoever upon the festivities. Leicester was the Disney of the times, planning sweet fun for his sweetheart Elizabeth, entertainments meant to please only for a moment. It was spectacular but frivolous. A performer representing the Lady of the Lake offered Elizabeth freehold upon her watery domain. I never forgot Elizabeth's retort, saying that she believed she owned all the lakes.

> We had thought indeed the Lake had been ours, and do you call it yours now? We will herein commune more with you hereafter!

How perfect. In the real world of *dramatis personae*, a real queen had a need and a right to assert her own preeminent existence.

At the dinners and dances arranged for the Queen, I had my first encounters with flattering rascals. I had seen for myself that my dress suited me and that my hair made my little face look far from contemptible, but only just enough that I could feel at my ease and examine the room without apprehension. Mother had warned me about courtiers attempting to seduce me, but I saw no immediate threat. The circle of ladies at court were so gossipy and complicated that few men made it past the flutter.

One exception was Philip's friend from University, Sir Walter Raleigh, who sought me out. Philip had said Walter would watch out for me at court; more to the point, I needed to watch out for him. To my surprise, when I finally saw him, he greeted me most inappropriately. "

> G'day, wench," he said, as he kissed my hand.

> I answered him in kind: "Mind your manners, whoreson knave."

It was a strange comfort that he reminded me of soldiers I had met at the taverns when I had been in disguise. Earthy words, even curses, were welcome diversions, not serious encounters.

*

Headline: Did Sir Walter Raleigh and Mary Sidney have sex?

Again, no, but wouldn't you have been tempted? I certainly was. But taught by the ancients, I had learned such fear of Rumour that it was much stronger than Bacchanalian impulse.

*

Put yourself in my situation, being 14 and going through a young woman's physical changes at court, amongst a coven of women eager to advise an ingénue on the expectations of her place. I was inundated with cautions and recommendations. Clothing, for instance they said, is no longer for play and posture. It becomes a metaphor for where you stand in the hierarchy of the court. More is more, but it is a mistake to don apparel that dwarfs a person's status. A collar too high or sleeves too puffy might signal where you want to be, but if it is far beyond your prospects, you look a fool. As a young woman, there is more to lose than to gain by over-reaching.

Prudent, trusting to the unadorned bloom of youth, I attended to these lessons. I took their advice about choosing court seamstresses, and I sought to dress simply, though I loved the fabrics and adornments so readily at hand, and I appreciated the skilful tailoring that could turn out so many variations on the folds and tucks to reveal surprising layers of colours and textures.

*

Court seemed intense and even fierce at first but the frictions were inconsequential in the end. Most in the Queen's chamber were kind. A lack of empathy did hold sway among courtiers jostling for preferred places, if you cared about fleeting favours. I received my share of slights. Momentary irritations could turn my otherwise contented day sour.

Elizabeth did not reward the infighting and I was of a similar mind, believing deep down that honour is earned, not sought; deserved, not given. Birth is a jewel but character is the setting. Surprisingly, though Elizabeth was almost 30 years older, we were of like mind about many things. She was a writer, and a keen observer of the ways of men and women both. And she could put herself in others' shoes, though the duties of state often curtailed how she could display her empathy.

At the royal court, Elizabeth was a pragmatist. She shared the belief of a fanciful dowager countess in a popular tv series today that principles are like prayers, noble but mostly irrelevant to the needs of nobility; rulers need above all to govern. Some of the powerful nobility held firm religious stances. Others cared only for power itself. The foolish saw their dreams in the spectacle of lavish excess. But Elizabeth needed to keep her eye on core truths. She took her duty as head of government very seriously. She asserted her power with force when she deemed it necessary to show who was in charge. She was Protestant to the core—that is, Protestantism as the sectarian core of stable government at the time. Religion functioned less as a set of pious principles, more as a bulwark against the machinations of the Spanish and French Catholic courts to gain power in England. I once tried to pin her down on her religious leanings.

"I believe in uncertainty," she said, puckishly.

Being cagey about religion was crucial in those days. I presented a devout appearance to others, even though my beliefs were anything but conventional. I prayed almost daily, and my public writings were only in the religious realm acceptable for women. In my private life, however, the distinction between Catholic and Protestant did not really matter. One of my best friends, Thomas, converted to Catholicism at a time when it could cost him his head. I supported him as I could, without losing my reputation as a devout Protestant.

In other words, the court was a constraint presented as a challenge. Learn to live within it, and make use of it, and it could be on your side. It would always restrict, but if you could see how to adjust, there was room to thrive.

Elizabeth took her maids on brisk walks regularly, and she allowed us the use of her magnificent library. She often sat with us reading. I remember when the first copy of Holinshed's *Chronicles of English History* arrived. I had only brief glimpses of it, and vowed to obtain my own copy when I was settled in a home of my own.

But the path of court life was not to be my primary interest. I could see that crowns were just another form of jewellery, a symbol of power but not power itself. Crowns were coins. Crowns were something to lose or gain. In many of my plays, crowns are something to give up: Titus and Julius Caesar both refuse the crown; Lear relinquishes it; Cleopatra and Marc Antony sacrifice theirs; and many kings in the history plays pass theirs along. Crowns are second-hand ornaments. Court would not be my life, but my life would always be lived on the periphery of the court.

You need to know how different that era was from the 21st century, in terms of the court and in terms of women, how different the parameters of life were, for me and for everyone. Those two contexts of gender and status restricted the scope of my activities all along but even more so later, after 1601, when my life and career would change in major ways.

I knew I would not choose to stay at court, even though Elizabeth at times became a mentor to me, a second mother to my youth. She understood my grief over Ambrosia, and gave me heart to turn my loss toward life. She schooled me to see that I had to know grief before I could embrace what I loved. It was a lesson I would fully understand only later. Elizabeth was wise.

The court was where I came of age. All the maids of honour were unmarried, supposedly virgins, and we were supportive of each other, understanding the significance and difficulties of the moment, and recognising what our status meant in the long run.

My second significant gendered moment, betrothal, happened after I had been at court for less than two years. Elizabeth was a compassionate, experienced guide to that event. Courtship and marriage are two separate events, she told me. She had known courtship that became scandal and she had had constant offers of marriage. She did not counsel me to follow her example. Her refusal to marry was not an option for the rest of us. She advised me to accept when I had a worthy offer.

11.   MARRIAGE

To honour my mother and my Queen I accepted marriage to Lord Herbert, an obvious and irrefutable choice for the continuity of family.

Uncle Leicester, the patriarch and great hope of our family, was the one who told me I was to be married. I was a 14-year-old maid of honour at court when he found me sitting on a bench watching the royal swans and reading, as usual. When he sat still for a while, eyes downward, without speaking, I knew something momentous was about to happen. Finally he asked,

> How stands your dispositions to be married?
>
> It is an honour that I dream not of, I answered.
>
> I have found a good match for you. Lord Herbert's wife recently died, after long illness, and he would like to have an heir.
>
> He's my father's age!
>
> Look to like, and see if looking move to liking. You will not be compelled.
>
> Good, my lord.

At first, I chafed at the loss of control over my future but as odd as it might seem in modern times, I did not have feelings of implacable resistance. For one thing, I delayed acceptance until my father and Leicester had approved the terms of engagement. As my uncle had promised, nothing would be forced. There were terms to be met, including property and timing. Arranged marriages can accommodate consent. "Thy will be done," the Virgin Mary said (for God's sake)!

I would accept the proposal but, as the fanciful Dowager Countess of Downton Abbey has said, "one way or another, every woman goes down the aisle with half the story hidden." My consent was to marriage, not to oblivion.

Everything in my family's experience showed that acceptance could indeed be uplifting, active not passive. Mother insisted that love is the stuff of fancy; marriage is the product of achievement. My family had ascended steadily to prominence, and I could add lift to that course.

Lord Henry Herbert was as honoured in society as was my father, though my father thrived in a more provincial realm. And Henry was almost as well educated as Philip. True, Lord Herbert, my dear Henry, was older, somewhat dull when seated beside my astounding brother, but he was a good head of household, as I would be later, after Henry passed. I never had any abiding grievances.

My chief reservation came from recognition that Henry's father, William Herbert, had been notoriously violent and unprincipled. He had slaughtered his own Wiltshire tenants who dared to object to his appropriation of their land; he had bullied the Privy Council and Parliament, holding out his sword before him and wielding his bullying voice; and he had betrayed my own grandfather, John Dudley the Duke of Northumberland; moreover, William had first knelt and kissed Lady Jane's hand as Queen, but then welcomed the Catholic Mary into London.

Henry himself, at his father's bidding, had rejected Katherine Parr, annulling his marriage to her, before he married Katherine Talbot. What was I to make of this shadow of violence and naked calculation of power?

But Henry was not like his father; he had been used repeatedly by his father in the accession games, and in his first two marriages. But now his father was gone and Henry was too humble to hold on to power. He had no greater ambition than to serve as an agent of the crown in Wales and in the counties around Wiltshire. He simply wanted a suitable wife who could manage a large estate and provide an heir. I did not admire him but I could honour his simple expectations.

*

Betrothed when I was 14, I married later when I was nearly 16. Father struggled for two years to pay an enormous dowry, but Leicester negotiated a generous settlement of properties to which I retained life interest: lands in Dorset, Wiltshire, Devon, Glamorgan, and Monmouth gave me an annual income of a thousand pounds, and I also had holdings in Sussex, Kent, and Surrey. There were hundreds of tenants paying me rent for such things as a mansion house, pastures, barns, meadows, and woods. I would eventually be a wealthy widow even before Henry provided for me from his estate, although at that age I had little thought for the distant future.

This was the time to seize the moment. I was about to become a Countess and I felt quite entitled to it.

12. WILTON HOUSE

Certainly, the Court overshadowed the lives of all my ancestors and heirs. We were attendant upon it. When I married and moved to Wilton, I gained a space outside the court but not free from it. I held sway in that space of my own, always aware that my space, like all properties, belonged to the Queen.

There was much fuss to settling in at Wilton House, near Salisbury. Suddenly I was in charge of a large household, with almost 200 servants, four times as many as we had had at Penshurst. Fortunately, extensive households and large account books were no surprise to me; I had seen Mother exercising control over the Sidney stewards very firmly. I would also rely upon my chief steward's assistance in managing the many lands of Lord Pembroke and my own settlement estates. Although Master Wilkins managed all daily affairs, I told him I needed to know everything. I had learned the voice of command from the best tutor, Queen Elizabeth. No one questioned me, as long as I did not question myself.

The buildings and park were under constant renovation.

> For me, I asked?

> Yes, dear, but Wilton has hosted royal progresses before, and we hope to be deemed suitable for Elizabeth to stay here as well, Henry said.

New stone carvings and stained glass at Wilton reflected Henry's interest in heraldry. His main belief was that nobility had a strong hereditary element, and mostly I agreed with that aristocratic bias. Where we disagreed was whether some behaviour was unworthy of the family advantages.

I can imagine a tormented soul wishing to change the circumstances to which he or she was born. For me, wealth provided freedom.

My family enjoyed wealth and power just short of royalty for about a century. It was a life of immense privilege, and I could not have written the plays I wrote without the advantages of many of the accoutrements of wealth. For several generations, status sat familiarly, though sometimes uneasily, upon our shoulders.

As to ostentation, we nearly rivalled the French court. What was conspicuous spending in my day? I shall catalogue it with indifference muting any glow of pleasure. There were jewels of course for extravagant display, rarely seen in daily life. They had little impact on the dramas of life on the edge of court. There were no lurid accounts of detective investigations of jewel thieves back then, thank God. Jewels were of value but not of consequence.

Similarly, foods were abundant and presented for momentary effect but they embodied comfort, not worth. Mostly the fare was similar to the daily tables of anyone with a solid income. The same kitchen fed upstairs and downstairs.

You will notice that there is very little in my plays describing foods, nor is there much about actual jewellery. Mostly you will find general advice: jewellery is useful as a metaphor or for colour, beef is for fighting men, cakes and ale for indulgent leisure; sweet things prompt indigestion. Personally, I was more interested in cooks licking their fingers and gardeners deciding where to plant strawberries than in the foods themselves. Food and jewels were just so many attractive but narrow things, too small for the scope of human potential. Boring in their physical manifestations. I was more interested in fabrics, as I indicated earlier.

And oh, our many properties were a joy to inhabit with tall towers and expansive rooms and porches. Knowing your place meant more than social distinction. We had endless spaces, in contrast to the cramped streets of even the most prosperous villagers or city dwellers.

Our place was physical, and sometimes quite idyllic. Wilton had fishponds, fruit trees, leafy walks, and a dovecote. We exulted in hawking and hunting in our vast meadows and forests. On our estates we usually saw no enemy but winter and rough weather. We rode to the hunt, our mastiffs uncoupled in the valley, marking the musical confusion of hounds and echo in confusion.

There seemed a harmony to it all, each in his place, unequal though that was. Philip and I loved the Arcadian expanses, the woods and fields and the riding and the leisure for us to immerse ourselves in a timeless space. A parade of guests and servants, music and talk supplied a panoply of activity. Philip delighted in the merriment and masking but he deplored the tyrannical, brutal act of hunting.

Time and comfort were the legacies afforded us by our ancestors. We slept in rooms with beddings and canopies of white satin and gold lace, and green velvet hangings. Tapestries bedecked the common areas with scenes on biblical subjects, especially of David, and also a set of eight depicting Romulus and Remus. In the great hall, light shone through stained glass representations of both royal and Pembroke heraldic emblems.

t was comfortable, but not always secure; it also a life of defence against uprisings. Our armouries stored enough Welsh hooks, staves, and other weapons to equip up to a thousand soldiers, ensuring our preparedness to defend the security of the region. For the nobility, we had armour; and, for display only, an Italian suit of damascened steel parade armour with a fifty-inch waist made for Henry VIII, given to my husband's grandfather.

n my lifetime we were not at war within the regions where we lived. For us, service to the Queen mostly meant travel. We were often on the road. In addition to properties in Ireland and Wales, where my father and my husband both served as governors, we had our primary dwellings at Penshurst and at Wilton, 100 miles apart. We were, in a sense, constantly on parade.

We presented ourselves as something very special, and to a large extent we believed that to be true. Even harsh experiences such as regime change and periods of disfavour at court seemed passing clouds. It is clear now in hindsight that we deserve to be proud of our achievements in literature in the Elizabethan Age.

must admit however that I am embarrassed now to see photos of the wealth still on display today, at Wilton especially, for so long my primary home. The supremely comfortable luxury of my span of days was part of the feudal arrangement that emplaced us as stewards of vast country estates (see Appendix B: Noblesse Oblige). The purpose was to manage with care, not just to recline ensconced in our own comforts. But during the following decades of my sons, grandsons, and on through the nineteenth century, comfort became obscene excess. There was a narrow sense of context in the succeeding generations, and too little focus upon the obligation of the nobility to be seigniors of the surrounding area, not just decorators of posh palaces. The patriarchs of my day, the first two Pembroke Earls, were at least aware of their communal responsibilities.

have now learned that my own sons, the 3rd and 4th Earls, began a long descent at Penshurst into display for its own sake. Subsequent Earls even outdid them in disgraceful excess. By the time of the wastrel 7th Earl, lavish self-indulgence led to such enormous debt that the 8th Earl sold off my precious books. The 9th Earl had exquisite taste at least, and he began allowing paying visitors in the 18th century to admire his display of taste and wealth. Today, you can see the craftsmanship of Chippendale and the landscaping and architecture of Inigo Jones and James Wyatt if you pay for a tour. But what vanity in 1885 to build a massive 600-foot-long stone bridge with Palladian pillars and architrave as no more than a garden ornament!

And an equally massive triumphal arch topped by an equestrian statue of the philosopher Marcus Aurelius—how ironic! Marcus would not be flattered: "the only wealth which you will keep forever is the wealth you have given away."

I am the pot calling the kettle black here. I ask to be judged by my deeds, not by the advantages to which I was born, and not by the excesses of my offspring. I do not think I abused my advantages. Nor in a way have the most recent Earls who deserve some respect for being steady custodians of a grand estate. They were born to opulence, and have laboured to become caretakers of it.

In the world I remember, every stratum was close. The servants wore our liveries and they had an assured place in the household. When the crown required a troop to be assembled, the command trickled down from the Dukes and Earls to the horsemen and the foot soldiers, all part of the same endeavour. We felt connected together, working and celebrating in very different ways, but part of a common purpose. No one lived in a vacuum; no one had a status fully apart, except the one wearing the crown, the guarantor of the security of all the rest.

13. PREGNANCY

Those first years of marriage passed quickly and nature took its course. Once it became apparent in 1579 that I was with child, everything in that wide household encompassing two extensive families revolved around me. I knew, however, that that phase would be temporary. Great responsibilities lay ahead of me, to care not only for the estate but also for my children, including, I hoped, Henry's heir. I was exhilarated beyond comprehension, in awe of what it all meant.

It was a relief to see that Philip, on the other hand, did not take my pregnancy so seriously that he lost his sense of amusement. Philip sent riddles to me for which the answer always was a pregnant woman.

> ...I'm an ode in nine stanzas.
> ...I'm a carriage, vessel, a stage.
> ...I've eaten a bag of green apples.

He was delighted with my eruption into adulthood, and in turn, I teased him endlessly with sonnets to urge him to get married.

> ...Thou art thy mother's glass, I wrote.
> ...Die single and thine image dies with thee!
> ...The world will be thy widow.
> ...You should live twice, in it, and in my rhyme.
> ...Make thee another self for love of me, / That beauty still may live in thine or thee.
> ...You had a father, let your son say so. (Even then, I knew what immortality meant. My words outlived both of us.)

I felt fulfilled, having set out upon building my own family; it would have been lovely to see Philip on the same path.

*

Residing at Wilton did not prevent me from staying close to the court, with the many advantages attendant upon that relationship. Ever since childhood, the Sidneys had been part of the Queen's Christmas family. She called my father by the familiar name, Harry. After my marriage, I continued exchanging New Year's gifts with the Queen. But my two families' closeness to the crown was in its twilight. The halcyon days of ease were terribly short-lived. Soon, my father, brother, and Leicester would lose royal favour.

The year of my first pregnancy is forever linked to Philip's exile from London. His mistake was sending a letter to Elizabeth in 1579 giving her advice not to accept a marriage proposal from the French Catholic Duc d'Alencon, whom she called her 'little Frog'. Philip reminded Elizabeth of her obligations to foster the Protestant cause. Perhaps chastened, she did not accept that marriage proposal. But she froze out Philip quite hard that year in resentment at his presumption in giving her advice.

Philip chafed at his inactivity at Wilton, having been trained for public service. Elizabeth turned a deaf ear upon his requests for a position in England or on the Continent, or in the New World where we had investments in Virginia.

Philip spent much time with me, often staying at one of my husband's properties along the Avon River, Ivychurch, a short ride away. I cherished the comfortable normalcy of Philip's visits, when we could ascend the hill behind Wilton to look across the woods and pastures to Salisbury Cathedral to the east, and Wilton to the west. Stonehenge was northeast of us but we were not then much interested in those monoliths. We talked of the bright future of English letters, not of the medieval or more distant past.

When I was six months pregnant, I retreated to the safety of Clarendon House, just north of Wilton, in quarters restricted to women. Nothing must imperil the birth of my first child. I made an exception to the restrictions to allow Philip to continue visiting, on the condition that he bring something new each time. That was when he began composing *Arcadia*, devising it as a tale to amuse me and the female household waiting upon me. It is the story of two young princesses being wooed by two young princes. Although I was not exactly flattered by his condescending tone toward his female audience, his *Arcadia* was dedicated to me, quite appropriately, as first auditor and also an occasional contributor.

Wilton was our Arcadia, our private garden of delights.

14. CHILDREN

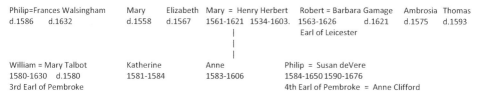

Philip=Frances Walsingham	Mary	Elizabeth	Mary = Henry Herbert	Robert = Barbara Gamage	Ambrosia	Thomas
d.1586 d.1632	d.1558	d.1567	1561-1621 1534-1603.	1563-1626 d.1621	d.1575	d.1593
				Earl of Leicester		
William = Mary Talbot	Katherine		Anne	Philip = Susan deVere		
1580-1630 d.1580	1581-1584		1583-1606	1584-1650 1590-1676		
3rd Earl of Pembroke				4th Earl of Pembroke = Anne Clifford		

My first child, William, was born in April, 1580 when I was 19, to the absolute delight of Henry, who at 50 had become quite impatient to have an heir. A wet nurse was employed and visiting godparents hovered over this most important addition to the family. Things had changed, utterly, beyond my control.

I know not why I felt so sad then; I had much ado to know myself. First there was me, an exuberant adolescent on the adventure of a new marriage; then there was the intimacy of a child in the womb, surrounded by care and attention, and then suddenly everything seemed on a path curving away from me.

Katherine was born a year later, then Ann when I was 22, and little Philip a year after that. The pattern held true for each pregnancy: there would be an interval of time when I could enjoy my brother's company and exult in the writing life; then confinement, birthing, rinse, repeat. In all, I birthed four children within five years.

I lost Katherine in 1584 when she was three, just as Mother had lost her first daughter Mary. But I had little Ann to care for, and Philip was a newborn. It all happened so fast that events overlapped each other, joy and sorrow intertwined. My love for my children was absolute, but much of their daily care was out of my hands, tended to by nurses and servants. That was the normal arrangement, not unexpected, and not unwelcome; yet the flurry of caretakers created some distance between me and Henry and the children. Caring for the children was a lifetime occupation, but not always an occupation for the moment. I needed my own pursuits.

15.   WORKING AT WILTON

Henry was a generous patron of learning and scholarship, and an avid collector of manuscripts of genealogy. His library was a delight and I looked forward to filling more shelves. Yes, I could finally have my own copy of Holinshed! Holinshed was often my guide, but he did not help me with something I constantly puzzled over. What were people really thinking when they behaved in surprising ways? There must have been doubts and uncertainties behind their decisions. I had more than one side, and it must be so for all others. I wanted to reveal the smouldering fires that tempered behaviour.

Henry and I both ordered books from London as soon as we heard of them, including *Marc Antoine* by Robert Garnier, with a fascinating portrayal of Cleopatra. I began translating it while Philip was there. Philip and I also began working on translations of the *Psalms* of David. He and I had grown up hearing the psalms as they had been translated from Hebrew to French by Clement Morot. I loved writing; it was as though I had another life there, or many lives.

In other words, I was already a writer by my 20's, working on serious pieces and being guided by the finest mind and hand of our times (while WS was still an apprentice glover). Philip and I were collaborators. I had the best of tutoring as well, to learn the traditional forms of verse from Philip and from his friend Fulke Greville, whom Philip and I had known since childhood. The three of us had been presented to Elizabeth at Kenilworth. Fulke and Philip became my tutors, because they had been trained at university in poesy, whereas I had not. I learned from them, but I also bedevilled them with my challenges to their every conventional prescription.

*

Philip's most productive years as a writer were 1577-83 while he waited for further advancement. He wrote constantly. He had decided to go in a counter direction to the one taken by Edmund Spenser, who drew upon Chaucer for a quasi-medieval vocabulary. Philip wanted to rely more upon contemporary English, retaining its connections with Latin, Greek, and even French. I was often his first reader and his quick foil. He valued my input but my suggestions mostly fell on stony ground. I felt that his writing lacked the intimate personal touch, and that his Arcadian impulse was based on medieval assumptions.

Philip finally married in 1584, to Barbara Walsingham, after his hope to become Leicester's heir had finally been set aside once an heir was born to Leicester's wife, Lettice. By then I had already had three children. My fourth would be born a month after Philip married.

Sir Walter visited at Wilton too, asking me how I liked living at the nunnery, a bold reference to the fact that Wilton had for 700 years been a convent, and a pun on the common witticism that brothels were a sort of nunnery. I retorted that it had been chaste at Wilton these 40 years thanks to the Herberts, and would remain so as long as I was around to resist such men as Sir Walter. I added that I liked it better at Wilton than at a court where whoreson knaves such as he stalked the corridors.

> Ah, he said, I can't make the doors upon your woman's wit. It will come out at the casement, or through the keyhole, or fly with the smoke out at the chimney.

Finally in 1585 Philip was restored to royal favour, knighted, and made a cavalry officer for service in the Netherlands as an intrepid champion for the Protestant cause. This military excursion was an undermanned, foolhardy, fatal attempt to wrest territory from the control of Catholic Spain. Philip intended military experience to be a flower in his cap; instead, the flowers capped his grave.

16. MEDICINE

As Henry Herbert's wife, I was also introduced to the mysterious art of potions. Henry's previous wife Catherine had been an alchemist, and when Henry fell sick early in our marriage, I applied Catherine's keys to the still-room in earnest. I hoped to find remedies in its store of unguents and herbs and oils. I found more than I could comprehend: dried blackberries, anise seed, mint, violets, roses, mugwort, cinnamon, honey, hyssop oil and rosemary. The varieties of concoctions would have been overwhelming if I had not had able, wise women to rely upon, who had been servants of Catherine. Mother shared with me what she learned from the consultations she had had with the scientist and magus John Dee. I also had advice from Adrian Gilbert, half-brother to Walter Raleigh and a member of the household at Wilton where he supervised the laboratory. I learned enough to relieve some of Henry's symptoms, but cure for his ailments remained elusive.

Again, the garden and the stovetop appealed to me, more than the splendour of public events at Wilton House. Tinctures and cordials for various ailments were a constant need in any household. Parts of the garden were for show, other parts for utility. I spent as much time there as I did in the library. Being the Lady of a vast estate, with unlimited resources for the time, proved insufficient for the saving of individual lives.

There was so much to grieve for beginning in 1586. Babies lost, young men lost, Mary Tudor executed, plague on the wind, wailing into the empty spaces. And the Spanish Armada assembling off the coast, aiming to invade England. My parents died early that year. What's it all for? Where is divine justice, and where is divine mercy? There's only life to answer, and me to see and record it, as if I were Philip's extension.

17.   PHILIP SIDNEY 1554-1586

Now to the main point, for me, of everything: most sad loss of all, news arrived in September 1586 that my beloved brother Philip had died in the Netherlands. There, in his exhilaration after capturing the town of Axel, he joined a sortie to prevent supplies from reaching the besieged Spanish garrison of Zutphen. Deciding for the sake of speed not to wear his leg armour, during a skirmish he took a musket ball in his thigh. His recovery seemed on course until the wound festered.

Philip's death shocked England. He was the flowering of the English Renaissance, and at just 31 we all lost him. This death was a loss not only to me but to a nation. Philip was a born leader, but I say with some bitterness that he was prevented from being titled in his own country. He put himself forward at every moment when a leader was needed. Earlier, he had taken the risky step of advising the queen on her marriage plans, and for that he paid the price of a year of exile and more years of disfavour.

Stymied thus early in his diplomatic career, he picked up the lance in the literary arena. No one else could have asserted his voice so effectively. He led the charge to push English into a new phase of prominence, going in a direction that rejected the medievalism of our good friend, the genius Edmund

Spenser. He preferred a livelier, more lyric style. His delights were dolphin-like, immersed in a love of the physical world, rising steadily into ethereal wonder.

Despite being made a Baron in France, and being the grandson of a Duke and being the godson of a King of France, in a family that contained four Earls, Philip was an untitled commoner until 1583 when he was finally admitted at the age of 29 to the Order of the Garter in England. Even then, his title was not by royal preferment but only by a technicality as a stand-in for a German prince who could not attend his own installation. As his proxy, Philip had to be given a title himself. At last, he could be addressed as "Sir." Was it the Earl of Sussex who had thwarted him, or someone else at court? We could never be quite sure.

In his final act of loyalty and courage, he put himself forward again for the military action in the Netherlands, and fought bravely, as a leader. He was expected to become the future Governor General there. Everyone could see what an extraordinary person he was but his promise was ultimately left unfulfilled.

Leadership is an essential quality, as my plays show. A leader doesn't have to be a man; Elizabeth was a great one. But when anyone seeks leadership for its own sake, it leads to disaster. Great leaders are driven by a need that rests upon higher values. Nations need strong leaders, and men are given preference for that. If men do not step up, women might do so. But true leaders are few and far between. Philip was a great one, a noble life cut short. My grief was not only for myself, but also for the nation, for the arts, and for religion.

When his body was returned to England, I was able to hold some of the bloody clothing that came with him from the Netherlands, from the literal underworld. The horror was unlike anything I had ever felt. There was so much life in him, and then only the stains remained. Where had that power gone? It seemed quite simply lost. My sleep in those days was often disturbed, and I had thoughts of ending it all. I could no longer believe in anything with certainty.

He was memorialized throughout England. After a state funeral, his body was laid in a tomb at St. Paul's Cathedral. No woman was allowed to walk alongside his funeral cortege, but the sight of his crimson-stained garments was all the memorial I needed. The horror remained all my days.

I now learn from later records that the Cathedral burned in the Great Fire of London in 1666 and his tomb along with it. Sadness thus pervades even my virtual life.

In sum, his death in 1586 gave me a different kind of grief, far more transformative than my earlier grieving for parents, siblings, and children. Philip had been my idol when I was a child, and my double growing up. He and I collaborated in so many ways that it seemed he and I were two parts of a whole, more than the sum of its parts. On that level I missed him, but that was a kind of grief I had known before.

The deeper grief was that the world had lost something irreplaceable, a unique and powerful life-force that would never be seen again.

*

Upon the news, I returned to the Pembroke home, Wilton House, to grieve and to await the ceremonies of the return of his remains. I cursed the senseless waste of war. All the hope of youth seemed lost. Entire days drifted by in searching step by step, crumb by crumb, for the fragments of my childhood, youth, early marriage, and adulthood. Philip had always been within reach until now.

> After a restless night, I rIse early to have the place to myself. In the glow of predawn, the sun strikes the low hills in the distance. Everything is draped in a golden quiet.

I stare out the gate into the shadows in the woods, a dense green that would take on a blue tinge toward evening. Something had come to an end. What was it, though? And what was beyond?

I decide to venture out on my own on horseback, something I almost never did alone. But there is too much inside me to be contained within the walls of Wilton. I know the roads and I know the dangers at the moment are negligible. I set out for Stonehenge. I disturb Chalkhill Blue butterflies and white admirals as I ride. I see fat coneys feeding on the short sweet grasses.

The ruins at Stonehenge had very little appeal for us in our era when England was seeking its place among the powers of the Continent. We English were often dismissed by the French and Italians as barbarians, little more civilised than the combative Scots and Irish clad in animal skins. Those ruins seemed to represent only what we had lost. We writers in English placed our hopes in the future, not the past.

But could the ancient site tell me anything about bygone hopes? Philip was gone, but does loss preclude hope?

It takes over an hour to ride there, over dirt roads that have seen little use.

How beautiful the stones are! How soft the light. How cold the dew on the edges of the grassy ditches! The stones rise up in the morning light, seeming to express a longing for things beyond the present. I circle the ruins, imagining the people who had dragged these enormous stones into place from somewhere distant. I feel the power they believed dwelt here, a power fuelled by their belief and by the enormity of their construction, their evocation of power itself.

What would they think, if they could see these ruins now? Would the builders feel their efforts had been pointless? Would the priests lose faith?

No, the site had been magnificent and remained so. The joy and the power never decayed, only the stones themselves.

Up here on this flat plane, am I feeling the diminishing impact of the cruel blow of Philip's death and sensing it fading away? I dismount and walk around and around, daydreaming in the wind that almost freezes my lips, tracking with my eyes the way the stones capture light.

Had Philip's life and work been pointless? Had we been pouring ourselves into a vain hope doomed to fail? No, his work must be honoured.

Then, decisively, I know what I want, a future that includes my own hopes and Philip's promise of greatness, a future that will erect memorials to his spirit. I mount my horse and climb back into the woods whose crests are now tipped with fiery rose. Onwards!

I return home well before midday, exhausted and ravenous. I eat in the kitchen with the servants, taking sheer delight in the flavour of crisp, crunchy bread and a juicy costard apple. I feel humbled to be the mistress of this household, charged with a responsibility to the land and the community,

Wilton now means both grief and duty to me. I will work now toward the future.

18. GRIEF

Losses continued, of the usual kind. We lost the family patriarch Robert, Earl of Leicester, two years after Philip. My brother Thomas died five years further on, and my husband almost a decade after Thomas.

My husband Henry lingered for months until the winter of 1601, leaving me then a Dowager, with stability but most importantly, still with a voice. I cared deeply for Henry, as my loving and capable husband, and master of the household. But Henry was 25 years older, and quite ill from 1596 until his death early in 1601. He had been bedridden for over a year before; I brought him frivolous speeches from my comedies to entertain him. He loved the fanciful evocations of Titania and Oberon. I honoured and entertained him, but I had no quarrel with Death on his account.

Mine was a life punctuated by a terribly ordinary string of losses in the closing years of the sixteenth century, but only Philip's was an engine of significant driving power to generate a steady current for my writing. His good remembrance lie richer in my thoughts than on his tomb.

These several griefs, and my particular woe, constituted a conflagration, out of which my second self could arise, phoenix-like, to emerge as a fully-fledged author.

Now, I am able to tell the whole tale. I will take you down the hidden lanes around the corner from the public arena. Those lanes lead back to the origins of ny work as a writer, the first of which is the emotional spring from which the iver of words flowed. That first welling up of words sprang from grief.

Ask yourself what on earth prompted a young Duchess to translate the *Psalms* hat Philip had begun, and then to translate French drama; and what caused her ater on to convince her husband to sponsor the London troupe of Pembroke's Men? I had a driving purpose, my desire to honour my brother worthily.

Ask also whether it made sense that I seemed to lead such a silent life from 1590-1613, after writing furiously during the five years before then. Me, silent? nconceivable. Open your eyes dear Reader and prepare to be illuminated.

19.   RENEWAL

There was a great national sense of grief after Philip died, but comfort there was none, for me. Friendly condolences were more moribund than the dead hemselves. Oh, poor thing, losing your mother, you have my sympathies, and your brother too, such a rising star, what a loss. Over and over again, for a year and more, I heard these commiserations. But true grief lay elsewhere, that within which passeth show.

Gradually, day-by-day, I rose to myself. One respite was sport. Hawking, riding, and archery calmed me. In childhood, those activities were manageable challenges; the weapons master at Ludlow Castle in Wales often complained hat my arrows had lodged in the parapets instead of lofting over and beyond. kept trying.

Ludlow Castle 1852 (Wikimedia Commons British Library Mechanical Curator Collection)

Now, the arrows easily found their higher course, and so would I. Physical activity reminded me that my only choice was to loft my own arrows each day, to rise and say "I, Mary Sidney...." These transformative arrows had to be of my own launching, my own flight in place of the aspirations of my brother. I hardly considered where those arrows would land. I simply had to launch them.

Over the horizon, though I could not see it at the time, would be much splendour.

The Winter of despair gave over to the Spring of hope. We always looked forward to the daffodils and primroses. The refreshing winds of March and the return of the swallows lifted our spirits. And the gardens replenished our alchemical laboratory, where possibility pooled in every flask.

Upon the return of this Spring, I looked at the psalms Philip had begun translating, and I found comfort in Psalm 73: "to sing His works while breath shall give me space." Psalms seem to me less about worship than about basking in the full splendour of the creator's world, and submitting to the vagaries of fate. I was not yet 25 and uninclined to dwell in the past. I would sing the glories, amusements, conflicts, confrontations, and resolutions of this world as well as I could, with Philip beside me in spirit.

I knew deep in the experience of my family's disappointments that renewal of spirit was what I needed; in the opposite direction lay tragic hubris. The misjudgement of assuming godlike power over momentary circumstances is the error made by characters I would later describe: Macbeth, Lear, and Coriolanus.

God's world included battles and deaths. I set about to observe the realms of politics and personal interactions as if I were God's spy, recording and reporting the conditions in the contentious arena of courtly preference, singing His works faithfully and unsparingly.

There seemed uncertain purpose in life's losses, but always a will to create upwelled in me, yearning for more vibrant form, and in my writing I could raise something out of those depths. Everywhere I saw loss transformed, in gardens and in families and in individual lives, both the torment that grew with time and understanding and the exhilaration of catharsis, the release of powerful emotion.

Dr. Moffett at Wilton advised rest, but Philip would never have simply rested. My grief weighed heavy, but not chokingly. Grief over my brother's death bid my o'er-fraught heart give sorrow words. In my darkest hours of rage and despair, I immersed myself in projects of writing.

There was a seventeen-year interval that was especially mine between three significant deaths: Philip in 1586, my husband in 1601, and the Queen in 1603. Those seventeen years were my apprenticeship as an author. For that interval, I was free to follow my own course to an extent; afterwards, I had to act more circumspectly.

Grief, how to move on: what to do? After some months, as spring turned to summer, my desire to honour Philip firmed into the certainty that I must continue to write, more and more ....

20. "SONNET 18"

I wrote sonnets all my adult life, with no thought of publishing them. The sonnets circulated in handwritten form among friends. Several of my sonnets were written when Philip was still alive, to encourage him to marry in order to pass his image on to the next generation through his children. I like to think it was due to my pleading that he finally married in 1583 at the age of 29.

Then In 1609 someone obtained copies of my sonnets and published them for profit. I didn't mind. I had no hand in the sequence assigned to the sonnets. The sonnet labelled #18 in the book is usually taken as a love poem. It is that, but the love is for my lost brother. It expresses my resolve to create lasting tributes to him in words. Philip was caught short in the summer of his life, and that made his life a glorious, undimmed summer's day.

> Shall I compare thee to a summer's day?
> Thou art more lovely and more temperate:
> Rough winds do shake the darling buds of May,
> And summer's lease hath all too short a date;
> Sometime too hot the eye of heaven shines,
> And often is his gold complexion dimm'd;
> And every fair from fair sometime declines,
> By chance or nature's changing course untrimm'd;
> But thy eternal summer shall not fade,

Nor lose possession of that fair thou ow'st;
Nor shall death brag thou wander'st in his shade,
When in eternal lines to time thou grow'st:
   So long as men can breathe or eyes can see,
   So long lives this, and this gives life to thee.

Philip would live in my words. If I could write well enough, we might even share immortality. As Petrarch said, fame conquers death, and in my case, it even conquers time.

My resolution to write as a tribute to Philip mirrors one of the dominant themes in my plays, a belief in the power of transformation. At our best, we can convert devastating failure into glorious triumph. Even at our worst, after every defeat, a new regime arises, in defiance of our misery.

*

I believe deeply in the Christian concepts of conversion and reform. My earliest plays, especially in the comedies, reflect those beliefs. I also exhibit the alternative in *Titus Andronicus*, where faith in transformation is not in the Roman code, and as a result none of the characters transcend their injuries.

Christian trust in change on the other hand even allows an attempted rapist in *Two Gentlemen of Verona* to recognise his error and be allowed to marry his intended victim. Neither that play nor *Taming of the Shrew* appeal to the tastes of 21st century audiences, but then, this is not a very Christian century. In the 16th century, we not only believed in transformation, we waited patiently for it. The best example of transformation is the my later play, the currently more popular *Henry 5,* where the wastrel Hal becomes the greatest leader in English history.

Grief is just one of the temporary feelings of defeat or loss which ought not in itself be a stopping point; it is a powerful incentive to generate something restorative.

Only if we can attain the projection of our better selves...

Part of my personal aim to be my better self was to master the tools of language. I knew words, but I did not yet know much about the rules.

Between 1586 and 1588, I intensified my study of the mechanics of poetry, using David's *Psalms* in particular to practice those forms. Philip had finished translating 43 psalms so there were 107 to go. He set the warp, and I weaved the web to its end. I loved the puzzle of how to put them into contemporary English. I took Miles Coverdale's translation and the French psalter and the *Geneva Bible* as my bases, as well as Latin sources.

My translations were meditations, focussing on essential principles. There is much in the psalms about righteous vengeance, for instance, as my uncles knew when they translated psalms in prison. There is also much about jealousy and slander, vices seen often in the enemies of my family, people who were envious of us and who seemed to inhibit our just deserts. Yet I felt uncomfortable with the emphasis in the psalms on enemies. The harsh division of power into friend and foe seemed to miss the point of reliance upon divine justice. I saw more healing in the psalms than vengeance.

It was a very productive two years, furious even, fuelled by all the burning energy of my grief, in a space without distracting diversions. Unlimited candles and dutiful servants attended many late-night sessions of study and writing.

Isolated in Wiltshire, I removed myself from London society for two years but not from literary society. I regrouped the circle of writers Philip and I had been patrons of that included Samuel Daniel, Thomas Campion, Fulke Greville, and Edmund Spenser. One participant, Walter Sweeper, said that Wilton was a little university, a nursery for learning. We shared ideas on how the English tongue could become more literary, and more universal in its appeal.

On many accounts I hold myself beholden to Abraham Fraunce. He had been working with my husband to codify the rules of law to aid Henry in his new role as chief magistrate of the wide jurisdiction of Wales. I respected Fraunce and his expertise immensely, having grown up seeing law courts held at Ludlow and in Dublin. Father's apartments were a living courthouse; lawyers and witnesses were practically resident. At Ludlow, there were even gallows nearby. In a way the law was the same territory as writing, using similar materials such as declarations in the form of indictments, and detailed accounts of demonstrative actions.

I was proud to be Fraunce's prize student. He had the ability to apply his organizational and conceptual skills on legal matters to a literary territory as well, codifying the rules of poesy. He published *The Arcadian Rhetoric* in 1588. To the utmost of his ability Fraunce supplied me with all necessary instructions and directions to become a poet. With Fraunce's help I explored the forms of poetic verse, devising 126 different rhyme schemes for my 107 psalms, culminating in my *tour de force*, Psalm 119 with its 22 different stanza forms.

I finished most of these translations during my two-year retreat at Wilton. Translating psalms had significant political consequence; French writers were calling upon Protestant translators to be burned as heretics. I kept revising them in odd moments and finally presented a printed copy of the *Psalms* to Queen Elizabeth in 1601, when she was near death and the religious issues had become more settled. I wanted her to know of my achievement. My family had long seen the psalms as an expression of the Protestant faith, and I was proud that these translations added my voice.

Mary Sidney holding a copy of her Psalms (Wikimedia Commons)

https://trinitycollegelibrarycambridge.word press.com/2019/03/08/the-sidney-psalms-and-mary-herbert-countess-of-pembroke/

Writing filled my days. I edited Philip's *Arcadia* and brought it to a state ready for publication. My edition became the most popular work of fiction for 200 years. I also worked on my translation of *Antonius*, a closet drama I liked for its attention to the viewpoints of both noble protagonists and their subjects. and I wrote original poems, "The Lay of Clorinda," "Angel Spirit," and "A Dialogue between two shepherds," a nod to Philip's love of the pastoral style.

But I needed more than translation, more than imitation. I knew that my own voice was something outside the norms of contemporary literature. In particular, I saw dramatic dialogues and monologues as my best forms. To make my own path, I began writing plays, seeking to transcend my bitterness. I needed to show myself to be a worthy successor to Philip.

Philip preferred the pastoral form. I, on the other hand, sought not just pastoral lyrics but the expression of those lyrics through the medium of characters' personae. Fulke and Abraham urged me to take up Philip's lance and write in the Arcadian mode. No, I said. Although I see much truth in Philip's vision, he was bound by the idealistic spirit of the landed gentry. He and I and my family lived some of the Arcadian ideals; we shepherded our abundant resources for peaceful ends. But I do not see the world the way Philip saw it. The Arcadian style does not seem well-suited to harsher emotions such as grief. I had hard truths to express, especially the bitter fruit of sectarian divides, the kind that killed Philip.

*

Grief, how ought I to move on? How ought I to espouse life, and denounce the forces against it? Writing kept me aligned with the forces of life, and at the same time it kept Philip alive. I could imagine him watching me, urging me on, as he did so often when we were devising entertainments at Penshurst and at Wilton.

Beginning even before Philip's death, from the age of 20, I had found a talent as a translator. Words were my sustenance, in any language I could learn. Translation was acceptable women's work, so I revelled in the freedom to reveal publicly my ability to capture the subtleties of *Psalms*, French drama, and Petrarch.

Some have said that I would have been so completely preoccupied with my responsibilities as a mother and as the Lady of a large estate, that it must have filled my days, leaving little time to write. Not so! Writing is a matter of focus, not time. The tasks of moving household between London and Penshurst were a familiar sequence, repeated continuously during both my childhood and adulthood. It was a brief flurry for a few days, requiring very little concentration, and then finished. Servants took care of the matter from beginning to end. As for daily management of the estates, stewards oversaw every aspect. Has anyone seen Upstairs/Downstairs? Our every need was seen to, and our word was law. We had more free time than you could imagine.

The proof is in the records: After Philip's death, with birthing behind me and family diminished to a focus on my two sons, I translated psalms and other works, edited Philip's *Arcadia*, wrote dedicatory poems, and kept up a literary salon. That same productivity continued for 25 years. A burning ember of grief pushed me, hardly ever sated, except in moments giving body to the positive forces of transformation, reconciliation, and the sheer joy of being immersed in a stream of true words. I translated copiously for over a year, and then began to concentrate on drama.

For 14 years a child; for 13 years a young adult: everything before I was 27 was my youth. Marriage, children, fumbling efforts at writing, all a part of the nascent self. With the death of Philip and of my parents, my full adulthood began to emerge from the chrysalis. Just ahead, my maturity.

PART THREE: 3RD self 1588-1613

22. LONDON 1588

In November of 1588 I made a triumphal return to London in time for the celebrations planned for Accession Day to honour both the Queen and the divine intervention that sank the Spanish Armada.

I spared no expense. For the journey from Wilton I sat in a coach led by a train of forty gentlemen on horseback, two by two, all finely dressed, wearing gold chains. Behind me were another coach and a litter for the children, and then another train of forty servants on horseback in the blue family livery.

I was back, swathed in splendour. But I did indeed have that within which passeth show. I had my mother's voice and my brother's love of words and my husband's and father's efficiency and, courtesy of Queen Elizabeth, the security of a nod of support at court. She knew my grief, and she knew my writing endeavours, and she would have my back.

*

My progress into London marked the moment I fully understood that Philip's loss was my license, allowing a kind of freedom despite several restrictions imposed upon women. Moreover, when Leicester died and then his brother Ambrose not long after, it was left to me to speak for the noble achievements of the Dudleys. It would have been Philip's role to claim, but I was the last one standing.

First, the formalities. Women were not permitted to participate in his funeral procession, supposedly one of the grandest funerals in living memory. Another convention was the obligatory year of grieving, so I kept to myself for not one but two years, after which it was acceptable to make a spectacular return to London. Mourning had only a brief space in the public mind easily replaced by spectacle.

Second, I had not been invited to contribute to a book of elegies for Philip, although it was respectable for me to finish his translations of *Psalms* and circulate them privately. Once again, I did what I could; I wrote what was allowed. I could also continue his Literary Salon. And within that Salon I could write privately in furtherance of his dream of an English corner in the City of Invention. Eventually, that license became my own assertion, in my contributions to the London stage.

I slipped aside the restraints of public expectations. I would write for myself.

I had a list of things to do once I was back in London. Fulke Greville and I put Philip's *Arcadia* into print. Publication of my own work would have raised a stink, but by indirection I worked my directions out. I circulated some of my own writings amongst friends, in the approved aristocratic manner. In the Literary Salon, we exchanged bits of writing and I was looked upon as chief patron. I had largesse to dispense and the contestants for it went through tiresome cycles of envy and rumour. Courtiers who wrote, or who were patrons of writers, brought gifts or dedicated their works, all the while whining about losing my regard. But my restless energy required more outlets. I began to write for the stage. I turned to English history as a source of ideas for my plays, with Holinshed and my own knowledge of the sad stories of the passings of kings as my guides.

OK, major shift here, from mostly documented fact to supposition based on known facts. As to the first category, there is no evidence to establish exactly when sonnet 18 was written, but almost everything else to this point is supportable.

From this point on, the record is mixed. My sponsorship of theatre and my relationship with Matthew Lister are established facts. But you only have my A.I. word for anything I say about my authorship of the plays. Whose other word can claim certainty?! Same goes for much of what follows. I can tell you what I was doing, but I cannot yet prove it.

23.   THE STAGE

My career could now begin. In my freedom, I would write or collaborate on over three-dozen plays in 25 years. It all seems like a lot, but I am not boasting. it is a fact. I was already 27 when I wrote *Titus* and *Two Gentlemen of Verona* in 1588. Between then and *Two Noble Kinsmen* in 1613, I wrote more than a play a year. I had the energy and the resources; WS could not have afforded the ink, paper, and candles, even if he had had the wherewithal.

If you had known me then you might not have seen the motivating spirit; it might have seemed I had left grief behind upon my triumphant return to London in 1588. Dig deep enough to perceive the implicit signs of torment on the trail of my actions, however, and you might discern the insistent root of grief beneath the flourishing garden.

I worked with Kit Marlowe on *Henry 6*. The real King Henry VI himself was unsuited to politics and war, and his weakness led to the devastating wars of the roses.

In the *Henry 6* plays, Kit wrote the bulk but I wrote Eleanor's speech urging her husband to be more of a man, and her soliloquy later saying "Were I a man, a Duke, and next of blood, I would remove these tedious stumbling blocks and smooth my way upon their headless necks." Eleanor is a ruthless character born of my anger and grief over the loss of Philip.

That character was the beginning of my exploration of what it means to be a man, and how a woman's strength is perceived otherwise.

I also wrote Queen Margaret's inspirational speech to the troops about the courage it took for her to make a dangerous sea voyage, donning armour and leading an army:

> What though the mast be now blown overboard,
> The cable broke, the holding anchor lost,
> And half our sailors swallow'd in the flood?
> Yet lives the pilot still...
> Why courage then! What cannot be avoided
> 'Twere childish weakness to lament or fear.

That speech was a kind of warm-up to the later play *Henry 5*, for Hal's speech rallying his troops before battle. The *Henry 6* plays gave me a platform for trumpeting my resolve to make my voice heard. I could weather whatever storms came my way, and plant my foot astride the world through art, through drama, through a representation of life that was larger than any individual life could encompass. I was not Margaret, thank God, but I had more power than most English kings. I had the telling of the stories.

Behind this play is the crying need for a true leader, such as Philip could have been. The *Henry 6* plays hinge upon the weaknesses Eleanor and Margaret see in their husbands, weaknesses that set up the carnage in the subsequent history play, *Richard 3*, which gives flesh to my intimate knowledge of court intrigues and the history of English succession.

Richard's successful seduction of the wives of his victims might seem astounding to some in modern times, unless they have read or seen the portrayals in a number of my earlier plays of male protestations of love all too receptively heard by female ears. Weak women disappoint me but they fall for loving reasons, and they mostly only imperil themselves. Weak men miss their best opportunities.

24.   PEMBROKE'S MEN: LONDON, 1591

By 1591, some fatigue settled in, after carrying the emotional weight of numerous changes in my family. Henry had been ill since 1586 and now was dying, our sons were rebelling, and the Queen was also ailing. Those changes did not overwhelm me, but they focused my attention. I had enjoyed translating psalms and writing occasional poems, writing *Titus* and bits of *Henry 6;* but I needed more serious work. Enough dabbling.

Decisions confronted me. What did I really care about? I was nearing 30, and not about to slow down. I was a woman with a brain and with exceptional abilities. Instead of whingeing, I would find more to do.

The first step of my new life fell into my lap. While I was staying in London, I attended a performance at the Rose theatre. Theatres were open arenas, where the audience could walk around, eat and drink during the play. They cheered, booed and sometimes even threw objects at the actors. After sitting in the balcony of the Rose to watch Hieronimo raging for revenge, I left the frenzy of the theatre and went for a stroll in the rose garden. I sensed someone standing in the shadows behind me. Bowing, Richard Burbage approached, wringing his hat in his hands.

Your Ladyship, I beg the indulgence of your time. May I approach with a plea?

As you will. You know I enjoy the work of your company.

Thank you, your Ladyship. The pleasure we take matches, I hope, your own.

My pleasure is more in the plots than in the dialogue. The characters speak as though they are the only ones listening. I could wish for better. What is it you wish to discuss?

You know my Theatre in Ipswitch, which is under lease to me but now the target of a legal suit. I am about to lose the Theatre, unless I can raise sufficient funds to meet the terms of the original lease. I am seeking a sponsor.

I will bring your plea to my husband. You know he has sponsored theatre in the past.

Yes, your ladyship. I am hoping he might resurrect Pembroke's Men.

Your idea intrigues me. If it were to happen, might I be welcome on the sidelines as Countess of Pembroke, while you prepare performances?

Indeed, m 'lady, we would be glad of your presence, respecting the pride of the troupe. Advice might not be well-taken by proud authors and actors.

I have in mind observing only. However, perchance I might seek to channel my observations through an actor whom I know. My family has some interest in the plight of one WS, who needs protection from prosecution for poaching in Stratford. He has not so far been allowed to enter the grounds of the city. My condition for helping you is that you employ him, and allow me access to converse with him. He must be given a place in your troupe, and papers to reside in London. He is a writer and I will privately channel any thoughts I have to him.

Understooood, m 'lady.

Kind Henry agreed to continue sponsorship of Pembroke's Men. Even in his illnesses, he provided me with a gift to last my lifetime. Between 1591 and 1597, Pembroke's Men were often on tour, but the centre of its enterprise was n London. The troupe did not find financial success, but went on tour in several seasons before pawning their costumes for the last time. The actors, including WS, then joined other troupes.

> Some background of theatrical history. Henry had set up Pembroke's Men decades earlier to sustain actors for touring in the countryside when London theatres were closed down for fear of plague. There was an interruption in 1572 when acting companies were suppressed by royal decree. Queen Elizabeth's purpose was to bring the actors within control of the throne. Her decree created a short hiatus.

> Then in 1573, my uncle Robert Dudley, as Earl of Leicester and the Queen's favourite, was able to obtain a royal warrant for his company managed by James Burbage to perform anywhere within the realm. The Earl of Pembroke, before he became my husband, was also able to obtain a warrant, and his company of actors were in place already before I married Henry in 1577. By 1583, Elizabeth had further narrowed the licences to two super troupes, including the Queen's Men and the Lord Admiral's Men / Chamberlain's Men.

> For a while, James Burbage had an insider's edge in that period of narrowing down, with Leicester as his patron, but by 1591 Burbage was losing the theatrical competition. He needed a patron for the continuance of his own theatre work and for his son Richard's acting career, and I stepped up, with Henry's blessing.

*

As a creature of the crown, what mattered most to Henry was his influence at the royal court, dependent on the good favour of the Queen. Fortunately, patronage of the arts was a proper courtly endeavour, and Henry always encouraged me in that pursuit.

Henry's main faith rested not upon theatre but upon William, who was just 15 when Henry fell ill. Henry considered it a first priority that I guide William in obtaining court favour. Queen Elizabeth once again stepped up to give the family a firm foothold on the future: she welcomed William to court. I wrote my pastoral poem "Astrea" in thanks to the Queen, to be performed when she visited Wilton on her progress in 1599. She did not actually visit then, but she heard my poem later, and agreed with me that the poem presented a useful argument between Thenot (representing allegories, the ideas that "are not") and Piers (representing the plain concrete truths of the Plowman). Elizabeth never took allegorical tributes to her very seriously. Although she was unlikely to see herself as a plowman, she liked to think she was closer to the plain truth than to abstractions.

And she did give young William a place at court.

*

Beginning in 1591, I spent much of my time at the Herbert London home at Baynard's Castle, on the Thames between St. Paul's and the Bridge. It was a musty old place, but it had a large enclosed garden and bay windows looking out on the reaches of the river. From there I had water access to the Rose Theatre, right cross the Thames, and later to the Swan and the Globe. Burbage's Theatre, a three-story drum of a building on the grounds of a demolished priory, was just up the road.

For the next decade, I had a hand in many productions, including ten plays which were published without attribution to any author: *Taming of the Shrew, Titus Andronicus, Richard 3, Henry 6 part 2, Henry 6 part 3, Edward 3, Romeo & Juliet, Richard 2, Richard 3,* and *Henry 4 part 1.* Those were my plays, for the most part, as were nine plays later published under the name of WS, with my silent approval, beginning in 1598.

25.   WHY?? HOW??

So here we are at the crux of this whole narrative, this A.I. autobiography: why and how was the authorship of these great plays hidden?

The *why* might seem obvious, and yet difficult to comprehend in the 21st century. The writing life was limited for women to private manuscript circulation, not at all suitable to be conducted in the glaring eye of the public in raucous theatres. England differed from France in that way: women were barred from the stage in England, unlike in other countries on the Continent.

In England, girls and boys were brought up separately from an early age, and that division continued in adult life: men held public positions of action and authority, while women held complementary social sway with many avenues for influence. Elizabeth was the exception, holding absolute power for decades, and she held tightly to that distinction; she did not encourage female rivals to her pre-eminence as an author, for instance. It certainly was not wise to put the family name upon the stuff of theatre. Especially if one wanted one's children to prosper at court.

As to *how* this subterfuge happened, the simple answer is that a few insiders collaborated with me in the theatre world and at court. I will elaborate on the court situation in a later section. In the theatre realm, the deception was fairly easy.

Henry did not know and would not have approved of how much I would be involved in Pembroke's Men. First, I provided Burbage with my angry diatribe against mercilessness, *Titus Andronicus*, without revealing its authorship. He also took the *Henry 6* plays on tour, great hits with audiences for their energetic battle scenes, but also for their strong female characters. The largest portion of the audience was always female.

Second, when Burbage set about forming Pembroke's Men at the Theatre just outside the City of London in 1591, I asked him discretely to assemble the best playwrights of the day: Marlowe, Kyd, Peele, Green and Nashe. I wanted to learn from the best, and maybe do them one better.

One of the first endeavours of this team was a play about the Civil War, called *The Contention Between York and Lancaster*. But they had little sense of how people at court speak amongst themselves. Using WS as my cover, I contributed by revising speeches in that play.

WS: A ROLE PLAYER

Now, about WS. Wasn't he the author of the plays? The proposition is so ludicrous that I will not deign to attack the case. There is no primary evidence to support it, as scholars have pointed out for over a century. Writers and academics have increasingly expressed their doubt about Will. [2]

WS had been arrested for poaching in Stratford, potentially a hanging offense, having killed rabbits, and perhaps a deer (for the hide, to be used in his father's glove-making business) in the park of Sir Thomas Lucy, an unforgiving man. But Lucy owed fealty to my uncle Robert Dudley, who loved John Shakespeare's gloves, as many of us did. Sir Robert arranged for WS to move to the City of London, a jurisdiction open only to those with valid credentials.

---

[2] Doubtabout will.org

When WS arrived in London, I asked Sir Robert to send him to the theatre. Obviously, this was a set-up. Will from the beginning was my shill. Why did one of many actors in London, WS, have such unaccounted success? The answer is something long suspected, that WS was a willing front; he helped me keep my identity hidden. He was less indebted to his own work for his renown and celebrity than to the glory and happiness he received from my pen. He was the almost illiterate beneficiary of my restless scratching to alleviate my grief.

As joint sponsor with my husband, I was allowed to see plays in development. I could ascertain when certain scenes fell short in their portrayal of behaviours at court, particularly in the lines spoken by women.

Cagily, I recommended to Burbage that the actor WS be allowed to revise the scenes of courtly protocol and etiquette, and to improve the language of kings and queens and how they ought to be made to speak, as well as to bring female characters to life—the sorts of detail that the playwrights could not have invented from their own experience. While new plays were in rehearsal, WS would bring me texts. I would add speeches to them, and he would bring them back claiming them as his own work. I used my knowledge of statecraft, the law, and even foreign languages to enhance what they had written. WS insisted to Burbage that he did not need attribution, because he was just doing his job as an actor, making some speeches work better. When I began to hand complete plays to WS, he simply refused to say who had written them. Burbage could guess, but he also knew to keep it quiet.

Some of the original first drafts of these speeches and my revisions are in the public record, though without my name on them.[3] In other words, though evidence for WS as the author of anything is almost non-existent, the evidence for my hand is beginning to surface.

26.　　WILTON 1601, DECEMBER

There were three seasons of my life, roughly divided into two decades each: childhood and youth, adulthood, and Dowager Countess of Pembroke at 40. When Henry died, I felt the loss deeply. The loss of a spouse is a form of love

---

[3] See excerpts from those documents in *Tiger's Heart in Woman's Hide* (Trafford Publishing, 2007) by Fred Faulkes.

with nowhere now to put it. It will always remain as an ache with no remedy. However, unlike with the loss of Philip, this loss did not lead to any form of new resolve. I would continue as I had been, as a woman accustomed to her independence and unashamed to be wearing her red hat, as Jenny Joseph would say.

My future after becoming a widow rested in my own hands. Henry had suggested that I retain as my birthright the Sidney coat of arms, likely to put me in a stronger light as a primary member of the Dudley clan than as the Dowager of the Herberts. When Henry died, I lost much excess wealth, but I was still administrator of the extensive seigniorial holding of the Earls of Pembroke. That estate included Ludlow Castle and the town of Cardiff in Wales. Managing these estates was my duty for a short time until William assumed full responsibility.

Cardiff quickly became difficult: there were violent local attempts to shake off the yoke of the Pembrokes. Amongst other acts of rebellion, there were jewel thieves, pirates, and murderers as well. You know how little I cared about jewels, but I was not about to be taken advantage of. I took the chief steward of Ludlow to the legal courts. They sided stubbornly with my former chief steward, who scoffed at me as a "hysterical female." I was not allowed to argue my case in person. I had to rely upon male friends instead, but they were not willing to take any firm steps for such a hopeless case. The steward was trusted more than the Dowager Countess.

WILLIAM, 3RD EARL OF PEMBROKE

WILLIAM, 3RD EARL OF PEMBROKE

My son William quickly and proudly assumed his title of Earl but while he was in disfavour with the Queen, he was not much help. Elizabeth's welcoming William to court had not helped him grow up. Just 20, William was not yet taking life seriously. It was a blessing that his father, my Henry, never learned as he lay on his deathbed that the Queen had thrown William in Fleet prison for a month for getting one of her maids-of-honour pregnant. When released, William was banished to Wilton for two years, as his uncle Philip had been 15 years earlier.

After Elizabeth died in 1603, William took full control of the Pembroke estate. I was relieved of most of my responsibilities at Wilton. William returned to court and thrived as one of King James's favourites. Little Philip also became one of

James's favourites. I introduced my sons to James during his visit on his first Progress tour from London in 1603. I like to think they and I fell within his favour comfortably after that lengthy visit.

But under James's regime, I became more cautious. He was paranoid about the evil of supposed witchcraft, and scornful of women in general. His court was also hedonistic, interested in its own pleasures more than in the well-being of the country.

Although my role regarding familial power was nearing its end, my caring continued, in that I kept quiet about my writing. I would never reveal my work as a playwright, for fear that it might tarnish my sons' status at court. The court held sway over all my life, and that of everyone connected to me.

THE FREEDOM OF OBSCURITY

The dispute with the steward in Cardiff had been an annoying distraction, but the legal tussle did not interfere with my writing; I could not even plead my own case. After 1603 I felt enormously freed, no longer responsible for running an estate, no longer a dutiful wife, no longer steering children toward the right way. I had been fairly free since 1591, when I began Pembroke's Men, but after 1601 I had no one looking over my shoulder.

Neither did a regime change impede my writing. When Elizabeth died in 1603, I lost a friend and protector, but by then I was under my own form of protection, an ironclad secrecy. Those few who knew of my playwriting were aware that the secret must be kept. The literary circle I had formed with my brother Philip and Edmund Spenser had expanded to include Ben Jonson, John Donne and John Davies. Others knew as well, mostly on the level of speculation. Few knew the truth, and even then, they only knew bits and pieces. Francis Bacon knew the most, and as a lawyer he also had the discretion not to let slip anything that might matter to a friend or to a potential client.

*

Neither did the unauthorized publication of my plays affect me. The year Henry died, 1601, was also the year WS began to take the plays to be published with his name on them. For ten years, my plays had been printed with no authorial attribution. The laws at the time did not prevent WS and the publisher from printing the plays under his name, and I saw no reason to stop him. He certainly knew of my distraction with family affairs, and that I cared nothing for the public recognition; I certainly did not need the small sums he was given.

What required me to continue writing in obscurity? First of all, be assured that it was by design, a well-executed subterfuge. It was politic to remain unacknowledged as the author, both for my sons' sake and also simply to retain my freedom to continue writing. Revealing authorship might even have landed me in prison, once the misogynist James became King. WS served my purpose all along.

WS by the way was still liable for prosecution for the capital crime of poaching until the death of Sir Thomas Lucy in 1600. He had been a pup in need of my feeding. After 1600, he needed his association with the products of my writing to become financially independent beyond the expectations of any other actor. Allowing him to put his name on my plays was a small favour. He bought his modest Stratford home on my dime. To me, his income was trivial; to him, it was a big step up.

It was fortunate that few people paid serious attention to me after Henry died. I was never quite in public favour at the court. I was dismissed as someone who was impetuous when excited, volatile when provoked. Even those who suspected something thought my role was merely provocative, not substantial. Rumours spread among writers about me, as a meddling bluestocking whose interference castrated the male essence of tragedy and history. How absurd: my "meddling" urged men to take up their proper space, but held them to account for their mistakes. The same principle applied for women: know your power but do not misapply it. I knew that the extent of my own power was best held in secret.

*

Headline: Did William Shakespeare and Mary Sidney have sex?

What?! Good God, no. Whyever would I? While he had been scraping by as a young glover apprenticed to his father, I had already been a prolific writer. A Countess and her glover? Save that for D.H.Lawrence.

Beginning in 1593 with *Taming of the Shrew*, and increasingly after 1601, I handed WS entire plays to deliver to Pembroke's Men and his new acting company, The Lord Chamberlain's Men. Some were plays I had written earlier, or that I would write for the needs of the theatre company for the season ahead. It all depended on an expectation of profits. The troupe had a stock of plays that had already appealed to the audience, worth staging again, but the audiences always craved something new. I discovered that could write one in a few months.

Unfortunately, my attempt to assemble the greatest playwrights of the time fell on the stone-cold reality of death. The five great playwrights I had assembled were only active for a few short years. Thomas Greene died in 1592 indigent, complaining to the end that Pembroke's Men had not supported him well enough. Thomas Kyd died young in 1594, and George Peele also died too early, in 1596. Thomas Nashe, my most vocal detractor, lived until 1601. I had not spoken to him in 10 years.

Critics have discussed several of these playwrights over the years as possible authors of the great plays attributed to WS. I can assure you that yes, indeed, some of them were involved with my theatrical endeavours but only for a few short years. Only Kit Marlowe was a true collaborator, and not for long.

Kit Marlowe, the best of the five playwrights, disappeared in May of 1593, a great loss to the theatre in general and to my need for a collaborator in particular. He had been in the Netherlands that spring, spying against the Catholic forces of Spain. His disappearance at the age of 29 was very like the death of my brother, a casualty of unnecessary religious war.

I continued to collaborate with other playwrights, always under the cover of WS. After Elizabeth died, I worked several times with Thomas Middleton, and later with George Wilkins and John Fletcher. I used WS to communicate with them and I trusted them to use discretion about the arrangements. I saw no reason to hesitate to collaborate. My ego was not at stake as primary author. I don't recall needing an ego boost ever in my life!

*

WS wasn't useless; he was actually a valuable resource for some of my work, coming from a different stratum of society than I. Often, I asked him to use his own words to represent how a tradesman or an actor might express reactions to a situation I had set up. He also loved to mimic the words and mannerisms of some of the women he knew casually, to put it discreetly. And just as important, he had a gift for how things worked on stage; with his assistance, stage directions became stagecraft. The placement of characters on stage is crucial to all the plays. Who is on stage, who enters, where they stand, it's all part of the art. We worked together for ten years before his insights came to full fruition in the actors' scenes in *Hamlet*.

WS was not someone I could consider a friend, someone in whom to confide and with whom to discuss the art of my plays. Francis Bacon was that confidante, my closest friend, and a collaborator on legal matters that often seemed at the core of the plots of my plays. He advised me on the way to finesse the ending of *Merchant of Venice*; and the legal standing of many characters, including battlefield issues in the *Henry 4* plays; how marriages resolved conflicts in the comedies; and the issues of justice in *Measure for Measure*. But he did not write any scenes or speeches. As a scientist, he shared my interest in potions, plants, and astronomy. We disagreed on the stars: he saw only the physics, whereas my characters often saw agency in the stars.

The first decade of my work in the theatre was frenetic but it was exactly what I needed. Bear in mind that I was under 30 when I began writing plays for the theatre, with no further interruption from child-bearing, but with all the incomparable energy of a young mother.

*

I lived or heard first-hand accounts of the sort of scenes I put on stage. Many of my plays reflect my own experience within the courtly realms they describe. I had specific knowledge of the weight of royal history, aristocratic in-fighting and Arcadian leisure. I wrote what I knew, using my imagination to invent scenes and characters to enhance the stage action. I borrowed and enlivened plots that came from Holinshed, and made contemporary versions of stories from the ancients. When it comes to war, my family is full of warriors; when it comes to men, I observe nothing has changed since Sophocles.

When I had to depict war, obviously, my imagination was stunted. I did not know armed conflict the way Homer did, and that's why my battle scenes are brief and favour psychological over physical detail. I knew intimately, however, the feelings that dominated the battlegrounds of status.

TO BE OR NOT TO BE

What I was doing had not gone entirely unnoticed, though it was not traced directly back to me, fortunately. Even so, the writers suspected I was behind it; they loved to complain about inexperienced hands sullying some of the plays. One of them, Thomas Nashe, complained bitterly. He even mocked the use of iambic pentameter, saying "nothing but to be, to be, on a paper drum." To be fair, it's one of his best one-liners. For the sake of humour, he was oversimplifying the technique. He had a point, that it could be a deadly rhythm in clumsy hands.

When I wrote *Hamlet*, I remembered his quip and decided to niggle the memory of Nashe with an Easter egg to immortalize his shame. But my version had a trick to it, shifting the march of a "paper drum" to something more dramatic by adding variety, in the spirit of an interior monologue.

Here are the five "feet" in that famous line: 3 iambs, 1 dactyl, 1 troche.

> To be   or not   to be, / that is the   question.
> U| U| U| |UU |U

If it had been purely iambic, it would have had six feet, and the word "question" would have sounded mock French: ques-ti-on!

So yes, I borrowed that idea for Hamlet's soliloquy, with wicked glee at having the last laugh over Nashe, who was still living when I wrote it. I heard that he was in the audience.

Queen Elizabeth, the master of deception, helped me set up the mechanisms to keep my name off of the plays. She even had all copies of Thomas Nashe's vitriolic complaint against me seized.

Perhaps his discomfort and that of some of the other writers was not only that someone had fiddled with their proud texts, but more so that the fiddling had a distinctly gendered angle. Of course, no one knew what sexism was in those days; they took it for granted that everyone could see that the sexes were ordered in a God-given way. It made them uneasy that a Countess could resist a King, or that an aggressive Queen could actually seem noble and powerful, or that virile, assertive noblemen could quickly face mortal or immortal peril. Still, they ought to have had the wit to notice that their own life experience probably contradicted the stereotypes often enough as well. The Wife of Bath wasn't the only strong woman about.

28.   MALE AND FEMALE, THEY WERE CREATED

Do my plays show that the author is a woman? In one major way, yes: the work shows my own gendered limitation. Early on, women had more stage presence in my plays than men did. Even though the men propelled the plots, the women were more interesting. Most plays have only three or four women, but what prominent roles these are! They do not fit the traditional, expected stereotypes. They are not on the sidelines, secondary. They are not simply tamed or untamed. They are perhaps the most vital characters in the early plays, and sometimes the main character even in the late plays. Portia, Rosalind, Venus, Viola, Margaret, and Cleopatra stand firm, not relinquishing their capacity to choose, albeit within conventional restraints. Even Juliet has more sand than most of the men in the plays.[4]

Truth be told, I could not find ways to enhance the male characters in the early plays, no matter how noble or royal. They are flat figures, myopically driven by a single humour or mania. They are action characters without much inside them except suspicion, a sense of injury, and envious ambition. Look in the early plays for long speeches of any complexity: only the female characters have a full internal life. The male characters are all about show, a flash of energy saying 'look at me!'

I plead guilty to the charge of writing about what I knew, the female mind; I knew male characters mostly from the outside. Nevertheless, I regretted my limitations; I liked men, and I liked what they did best, their capacity for decisive action, for camaraderie, for self-confidence, for joy, even for rogueries. I had grown up with a virile brother and a powerful father and I had a strong husband. It bothered me that I could only portray one-dimensional men.

---

[4] Take a look at the e-book *Women of Resolve: female characters in the work attributed to Shakespeare*

Titus, Petruchio, and the kings had all been beyond the capability of my pen to enhance. They lack a sustained capacity of self-reflection, of consideration, of purposeful resolve. In contrast, even the few villainous females know what they are after. The males waver in their purposes, indecisive, with the exceptions of the single-minded protagonists Richard 3 and Petruchio. Those two had temporary victories. Yes, you can win the crown, or win the hand of a woman, or outplay your rival; but how will you thrive after your victories? That's the theme of most of my histories and tragedies.

29.   BEING HUMAN

What the double losses of husband and Queen meant for me was that I was unto myself, loosed from most of my ties. It was a pivot point for my writing, allowing me to ask myself what I cared about deep down. What, in all my endeavours, meant enough to give it all my attention, now that my life was no longer so predictable, no longer dominated by court, husband, children, and household? Family matters still took some attention, but only on the sidelines. What I really cared about was what I could discover about the depths of the human spirit. What did it mean to be human? Not just female, not just a beneficiary of privilege, but fully human?

In general, my plays sought to create rounded characters, not woodcut stereotypes. One thing became evident when I began working with playwrights and actors: human nature is not one-dimensional. I knew I could do better than most of the plays being produced, where stock figures on stage represent only the characters' external actions and features, with one clear motive. Real people have more going on inside, a mix of emotions: uncertainty, indecision, memories, regrets, intentions, a weighing of consequences, monologues within the self.

I understood the breadth of humanity but it did not always show in my writing. For 15 years, I found it easy to create women fully, but difficult to create men with an internal life. My early male characters could each be summed up in one sentence. Titus Andronicus, for instance, is a war hero who deserves leadership but is unprepared for the destructive forces of jealousy and revenge. A simple portrait. Petruchio is a suitor who refuses to accept any sign of failure. Kings are leaders who are often led by others. Noblemen work to maintain status.

Men in my early comedies are often just foolish talkers with a singular biological or short-term political aim, using words to mesmerise. And although women are more complex in private, they are often reduced in their interactions with men to simple acquiescence.

Manipulative lovers and poor leaders are similarly single-minded, seeking personal distinction or gain. Good leaders, honourable men, and fully-fledged women on the other hand rise to a higher calling. There are a few early works with three-dimensional characters, such as Henry 5, Portia, Lucrece and even Tarquin, a disloyal man who fights his evil demons and loses. That sense of a character's complexity emerged gradually in my writing from those first years in daily contact with live theatre. Eventually, I began to feel confident to bring all types alive on stage. But always, gender differences were on my mind.

In Part Five, I will stroll through the gender issues in my plays. But first, to complete my own life history, I will explain how the sonnets came about.

PART FOUR: 4TH self 1614-1621

30.   Spa 1614, June

My most potent life lesson came from my greatest loves, when I came to realize that any attempt to control a relationship would inevitably fail, and could even crush it. These lessons are displayed in my sonnets. Much speculation has arisen about the sonnets being addressed to a man. Everyone assumes that WS wrote the sonnets; some conclude that he might have been gay or bi. Perhaps he was. I wouldn't have cared.

In truth, the sonnets are about my love for three men in particular. The first two are my brother Philip and my son William. My love for them led me to write 17 sonnets urging them to get married. Those sonnets were written after I had married, after I had fulfilled the Herbert family's hopes for an heir and a spare. I knew my brother Philip also ought to marry, and he did, but he died without an heir. My eldest son William likewise died with no heir. Ironically, those 17 sonnets did not achieve their familial purpose. In other words, I could not control their issue. Pun intended.

Sonnet 18 gives farewell to Philip after he died, a sonnet that has indeed given him immortal life in words. I could bid him *adieu* confidentially, at least.

Most of the other sonnets were written for my lover after my husband died, Matthew Lister, our family physician. Thomas Moffett, the previous family physician, and member of our literary circle, died in 1604. When Matthew Lister took the care of our family, I liked him immediately, but he hesitated to accept my approaches. He was falling for me as well, but he saw the difference in our social standing as a barrier. He did not want a scandal. As a physician, Matthew knew how to keep secrets; we never became a topic for public gossip. Our affections were deep and long-standing. We fell in love when I was 43, a few years after Henry died, and the year after Queen Elizabeth died. Everything changed for me then, in my freedom to pursue my own life.

Take a look at the following sonnets, and reconsider their gender origins. For too long, they have been read from the wrong perspective, as poems written by a man for a woman, or from a man to another man. As is often said, the simplest solution is the one that requires the fewest complications. As the engine of the sonnets, my relationship with Matthew requires the fewest convolutions.

"Sonnet 73"

Matthew was 33 at the time we became lovers, ten years younger than I was. It was not a terribly awkward age gap but it was something I addressed in several sonnets.

> That time of year thou mayst in me behold
> When yellow leaves, or none, or few, do hang
> Upon those boughs which shake against the cold,
> Bare ruined choirs where late the sweet birds sang.
>
> In me thou see'st the twilight of such day
> As after sunset fadeth in the west;
> Which by and by black night doth take away,
> Death's second self, that seals up all in rest.
>
> In me thou see'st the glowing of such fire,
> That on the ashes of his youth doth lie,
> As the death-bed whereon it must expire,
> Consumed with that which it was nourish'd by.
>
> This thou perceiv'st, which makes thy love more strong,
> To love that well which thou must leave ere long.

I adored him for loving me so much that our age difference did not matter. But I have to note that this sonnet was not apologetic. The images here present age in spectacular beauty, in memories of the songs of youth, and the glow of sunset, and the coals of a fire. I am very happy to be remembered in those terms. How could he not love me?!

"Sonnet 29"

Sometimes, I confess, I felt envious of those who had even higher status than my own, whose families were thriving in the ever-changing courtly world.

> When in disgrace with fortune and men's eyes,
> I all alone beweep my outcast state,
> And trouble deaf heaven with my bootless cries,
> And look upon myself and curse my fate,
> Wishing me like to one more rich in hope,
> Featured like him, like him with friends possessed,
> Desiring this man's art and that man's scope,
> With what I most enjoy contented least;
> Yet in these thoughts myself almost despising,
> Haply I think on thee and then my state
> (Like to the lark at break of day arising
> From sullen earth) sings hymns at heaven's gate;
> For thy sweet love remembered such wealth brings
> That then I scorn to change my state with kings.

Adopting the voice of a man came easily to me, after writing so many plays, and it seemed best for this sonnet. A woman could be a Queen by birth, but not by choice, not within hope. This poem is about aspiration and ambition, territory restricted to men. As a Dowager, I had lost much fortune, but that is not what this poem is about. Deep, true love is better than any wealth or status imaginable.

"Sonnet 116"

Matthew lived at my estate as the resident physician. This sonnet was written early, not at the end. Marriage was not possible under the conditions of my husband's will, nor under the constraints of social class. But Matthew and I saw no barriers to our love.

> Let me not to the marriage of true minds
> Admit impediments. Love is not love
> Which alters when it alteration finds
> Or bends with the remover to remove:
>
> O, no! it is an ever-fixed mark
> That looks on tempests and is never shaken;
> It is the star to every wandering bark,
> Whose worth's unknown although his height be taken.
>
> Love's not Time's fool though rosy lips and cheeks
> Within his bending sickle's compass come;
> Love alters not with his brief hours and weeks,
> But bears it out even to the edge of doom.
>
> If this be error and upon me proved,
> I never writ, nor no man ever loved.

Double negatives can be very useful to introduce ambiguity. I am asserting here not only that I loved, but also that I wrote. Another ambiguity in the last line is that the verb love can be active or passive. I did write, I did love, and I was loved.

"Sonnet 33"

True love is timeless, and free of class distinction. At least, that is so in the abstract. But, alas, I sensed for a time that Matthew was having an affair; our love seemed only to have been a passing glimpse of sunshine.

> Full many a glorious morning have I seen
> Flatter the mountain tops with sovereign eye,
> Kissing with golden face the meadows green,
> Gilding pale streams with heavenly alchemy;
> Anon permit the basest clouds to ride
> With ugly rack on his celestial face

And from the forlorn world his visage hide,
Stealing unseen to west with this disgrace:
Even so my sun one early morn did shine
With all triumphant splendour on my brow.
But out, alack, he was but one hour mine;
The region cloud hath mask'd him from me now.
Yet him for this my love no whit disdaineth;
Suns of the world may stain when heaven's sun staineth.

I suspected he was having an affair with my niece, the dark-haired Mary Wroth. Several sonnets refer to my jealousy. But Mary Wroth wrote a play published in 1621 explaining that the affair was only a rumour; in truth, she had had a clandestine affair not with Matthew but with my son, William. Her play put my mind at ease: Matthew had not been disloyal to me.

Mary Wroth's affair with William led to two offspring, a fact that was kept secret until 1935, thanks initially to my son's position as Lord Chamberlain to King James. He was able to destroy documents and control the recording and dissemination of all printed evidence. As he did later to cover my authorship of the plays.

I did not write new plays for a few years when I was enamoured of Matthew, but I did write many sonnets in those years, between 1605-1610.

31.   FINIS

The plays were a reflection of real life, the world I saw, looking from on high, removed from any quotidian concerns. I could observe the faults of men and women cynically. My final plays were reflections of the world I had seen all along, the real sides of love and ambition, not the ideal side I was living with Matthew. *Antony & Cleopatra, Pericles, Coriolanus, The Winter's Tale, Cymbeline, Henry VIII,* and *Two Noble Kinsmen*: all of these plays show the constraints the world puts upon our emotional and our public lives. Even our most cherished relationships are guided by circumstance. Count no man happy until he is dead, as Aristotle said. Even comedies end on a note of conditional celebration, with a nod to gods who must be appeased.

The sonnets, on the other hand, were from within, personal, blissfully unconscious of the context of the human comedy. The sonnets were in the love country, known to all who have been there. It was an Arcadian world, such as my brother Philip imagined, immersed in the most intense and heartfelt emotions. It was based on what was fair, kind, and true. Only the ideal existed, not the tainted reality of broken histories. I lived in that country with Matthew Lister.

He and I often travelled to the Continent, staying at Spa most of three years, wintering at the beautiful town of Mechelin in Antwerp, visiting the Archduchess Margaret of Austria. When we returned to London in 1616, we occupied the house King James gave me at Houghton Park, with its magnificent views for 20 miles in four directions. The last ten years of my life were both emotionally and physically Arcadian.

*

When I could see that I was nearing the end of my stay on this sceptered isle, I implored my brothers to set my plays in print with WS designated as author. WS had nothing to do with the publication, as he had retired to Stratford in 1611 and died in 1616. I arranged for publication of my plays in the *First Folio* dedicated to "the incomparable pair of brethren," my sons, William and Philip.

There is some irony to that. My sons accepted the dedication with smug self-satisfaction but they disapproved strongly of my name being attached to the plays, a decision guided by their sense of the court of King James. And so, the book was labelled as the work of WS.

Lord Chamberlain of the Household

My son William had been Lord Chamberlain since 1616; he was in charge of all Court entertainments and took the players under his personal protection. He had the power to decide which plays would be granted a license for performance. In other words, he could censor the theatre at his pleasure. And he did! Not only that, but he was careful to ensure that no

Royal Coat of Arms of the United Kingdom

records in the Chancellery contained any evidence or even suggestion of my authorship of plays.

asked two of WS's friends, Heminges and Condell, to see to the publication of the plays. They had been close to WS, and they knew him as I also saw him, a gentle and easy person, a genial drinking partner who just happened to keep delivering good stuff for the stage. Whether they ever suspected my role in the plays is unknown, but they surely must have had their suspicions.

The volume of my 36 plays was published in 1623, in folio format instead of the quarto format usual for plays. Eighteen of the plays had never been published in any form. Of the 19 that had been printed individually, only half had the author listed as WS. The rest had been put out anonymously.

*

Thus ended my glorious career behind the scenes. I did not so much seek to excel or even to entertain but rather to appeal to both heart and mind, with constructions that would have pleased my illustrious brother.

And there it is, dear Reader, my account of a remarkable case of mistaken identity, of a woman disguised as a man, keeping faith until her brother or lover can participate in the miracle of allowing her true self to surface. Sound familiar?

PART FIVE: THE WHY OF THE WHAT

In the previous sections, I have covered the *who* (me), the *what* (my life and career), the chronological *when*, the *why* (the purposes of my obscurity), and the *where* (all of greater England, not just London and Stratford).

I will now address in *somewhat* chronological order, the *what* and *why* of some of the gender issues in the plays themselves, my living heirs. On gender issues, I have always had much to say. My plays have been analysed in the past 500 years in thousands of books and treatises, many dealing with gender issues. Still, there is more to be said, especially with my female authorship in mind, that perhaps only I can elucidate.

On a deeper level, however, lies the essence of what made my plays so often gripping and timeless. Think of two actors on stage, and one chair. Their shared aim is to have the chair. That is the generator of drama.

For each character there is always something at peril, beneath the surface issues of status, power, and marriage. The best characters are striving to find their best selves, as I was after Philip's death. All the characters are aiming at something vital to them, something the others can provide, sustain, or take away. Even servants need something that ennobles them, such as loyalty or the dignity of labour. The best actors are always attending to the character's core needs. Some ambitious characters veer into ravines of error, mistaking a phantom for a saviour, like Stephano and Trinculo being overwhelmed by the clothing they find on Prospero's island in *The Tempest*. Some few act disgracefully but then find a better self. Some remain haunted by failures that arise from their own flaws. Some rise to discover their higher virtues. I looked to give each character an added dimension, a continuation into time or emotion.

Most of the following will make little sense unless you have read the plays, but you will see threads that weave each play into others I wrote.

TITUS ANDRONICUS

My first effort at stage drama delved deep into my anguish, to find a way out of it. *Titus Andronicus* takes its gory account of raw revenge and atrocity from Cicero, Horace, Virgil, and Plutarch, my main sources. My grief over my brother

Philip's death launched at first my own projectile of rage against his fate. I would have feasted on revenge if I had had the chance. *Titus* gave me a chance to displace and sate the anger. My most blood-stained play by far.

The victorious general Titus returns to Rome and is offered the throne, but he magnanimously refuses. Subsequently his rivals brutally rape his daughter, whereupon Titus naïvely allows his own right hand to be cut off as a sacrifice to appease his enemies. His decisions make sense to him in this merciless, transactional world, an ancient, remorseless world best left in the Roman ruins.

The gender aspect is indirect here, in the male tendency both to try to control events and to make willing self-sacrifice for abstract purposes.

For me, this play is a repudiation of the tainted illusions of noble ideals. Titus believes in the honour of Rome, just as Philip believed in the fight for Protestantism, as a rational repository of decency and faith in individual agency. Titus likewise represents reason; but step-by-step, inexorably, he abandons any sense of a higher court of justice, wrongly concluding that the only revenge and slaughter can relieve his suffering.

I also believed in decency, reason, and faith as values, but I ascribed those values neither to Rome nor to Protestantism. My faith rested in a higher realm, on the belief in human dignity and capacity for mercy.

The ultimate casualty is Titus himself, who offers his enemy's son in a dish of stew at a banquet. Titus mistakes the false for the true, from beginning to end. He reduces revenge to one of its absurd conclusions, in vengeful cannibalism.

Between the contrary satisfactions of revenge and mercy, the scales for me tip in favour of mercy. If mercy had been employed at the beginning of the play, or at several points within it, there would have been no tragedy.

EDWARD 3

Besides *Titus* and *The Contention*, another early example of my contribution to Pembroke's Men is a marvellous seduction scene in *Edward 3*, where the already married Countess of Salisbury, (my alter ego, in that Salisbury is near my residence at Wilton) rejects the advances of the already married King.

Please forestall your curiosity: this scene was not directly about me. I had certainly heard stories of the predatory Henry VIII but no English king was my contemporary until I was 40, and James never tried. This play draws upon William Painter's *The Pleasure Palace*. Now whether I had ever been seduced at all, that is another matter. But essentially this scene is not about sex, it is about abuse of power.

The Countess in this scene is in a tricky situation where she has to rely upon persuasion. She attempts to educate the King on the ethics of attraction, beauty, fealty, and integrity, the foundations of which ought to be considered sacred. She puts him in his place relative to established law, with an analogy to the King's coinage:

> He that doth clip or counterfeit your stamp
> Shall die, my lord; and will your sacred self
> Commit high treason 'gainst the king of heaven
> To stamp his image in forbidden metal,
> Forgetting your allegiance and your oath?
> ...To be a king is of a younger house than to be married.

Edward relents, unable to deny this onslaught of reason and virtue. His seduction is a blatant abuse of his position of absolute power. The King of Heaven has His own currency of virtue; and so, for Edward to "stamp his image" upon a virtuous married woman would be the equivalent of a treasonous act against God. Her eloquence is that of a Daniel come to judgement upon the elders who tried to seduce Susannah.

32.   EARLY SEDUCTION PLAYS

In several of my first plays I explored the role of male seduction rhetoric in shaping misbehaviour. It was a relief after the deadly history plays to take exuberant pleasure in depicting the heady interplay of romantic adventures. I see nothing wrong with seduction, as long as it is fair play. I always valued strength: strong men learn techniques of attack; strong women use techniques of resistance until they are ready to succumb. I learned to be wary as an ingénue at court, thanks to the teasing tutelage of Sir Walter Raleigh. Romantics might think I am on their side, but they ignore how many plays show the foolishness of love, and the necessity of a more cool-headed assessment of the foundations of marriage on compromise, contract, and social status.

TWO GENTLEMEN OF VERONA

In *Two Gentlemen of Verona*, two men are in love with the same woman, Silvia, even while one of the men, Proteus, has already courted another, Julia. The only solution is for Proteus to snap out of it; after a few slapstick moments of violence, he comes to his senses. That play is worth more revivals.

 It is highly amusing to me that, in the modern film *Shakespeare in Love*, Gwyneth Paltrow recites Proteus's ridiculous speech on love in all seriousness: "What light is light, if Silvia be not seen?" The movie completely misses the point that the speaker is a love-struck fool, named Proteus because he changes shape at the bidding of his affections. His affections take a dark turn later when his attempt to rape Silvia is interrupted. I give him a chance to transform himself at the end of the play. He makes a conversion to a better self, a process I believed in throughout all the plays I wrote.

The core of all stories comprises mis-takings, reversals, regret, and the direction forward. In comedies, the mistakes are resolved. In tragedies, the misapprehension of words prevents resolution.

Men can be such fools, yet they succeed in leading women into error all too easily. After *Two Gentlemen of Verona*, I then began *Taming of the Shrew* and *Romeo and Juliet*, putting female characters in central roles, and showing both the power and the limits of seductive male rhetoric.

TAMING OF THE SHREW

Taming, the next play I wrote, pits two powerful people in a battle for control. Kate resists Petruchio's demands fiercely, until at the conclusion she seems to give in to his rhetoric and manipulation. Petruchio seeks to tame her shrewishness into submissiveness, and appears to succeed. However, I left it deliberately ambiguous. Several of my plays end with women in an ambiguous situation that leaves the question open as to how their lives will proceed after the manipulated marriages. Kate's concession speech at the final banquet has layers that satisfy the men without actually revealing the intentions of the women.

My own experience of agreeing to marriage showed me that submission early allowed plenty of power later. If I'd written a sequel of the play, it would show Kate's eventual dominance. Actually, *Merry Wives of Windsor* is that later sequel. That's another play worth more revivals.

ROMEO AND JULIET

I must clarify the point of one of my most popular plays: *R&J* is not an endorsement of early love. *Taming* and *Merry Wives* might be considered to be comedies based on the real phenomenon of wives and husbands at odds. *Romeo and Juliet* on the other hand is tragic because the marriage never has a chance to face the real world. Instead, the rash behaviour of the lovers leaves them vulnerable to fatal misunderstandings in the fog of duels, plots, and promises. This play is mostly misunderstood in our romantic era. Both lovers believe in the truth of rhetoric, but the plot is a bald object lesson: love is a thrill with a deadly sting. No mature adult can see that play as anything other than a warning, no matter how much we'd like to take the lovers' side. Romeo and Juliet pay with their lives.

I lived that lesson from the opposite end, the compliant track instead of the rebellious one, in that I was married at 14 to a man decades older, after having heard for two years the flattery of courtiers. Might I, at some weak moment, have begun to make Juliet's mistake? You'll never know. Perhaps I never met anyone as persuasive as Romeo. But my arranged marriage had all the advantages I could ever hope for. As far as love goes, marriage boundaries are somewhat flexible. That is all I will say on that topic.

33.   PLAGUE: *"VENUS & ADONIS"* and *"LUCRECE"*

Nothing shows the unpredictability of life better than plagues. Our theatre seasons were often interrupted by fears that the plague would spread in the packed area for what we called the groundlings. Acting troupes left the urban venues and went out to the countryside, sponsored by noblemen in their great halls. They also performed in market towns to earn a bit extra.

The main plague year for me was the season of 1592-3. I retreated to Wilton to write two narrative poems, "Venus & Adonis" and "Lucrece." The women in those poems continue the paradigm I myself had set within all my early plays, of women remaining steady while men waver.

Venus fits one pattern I had seen among women: she woos while Adonis resists, a reversal of gendered expectations but just as common as male seduction. She demeans herself in language similar to words that Helena will subject herself to in *Midsummer*. Yet she persists. Adonis remains indifferent to her appeals, preferring instead to go on a boar hunt that takes his life. Really, quite a bore. We cannot miss him, but Venus does. The poem is in the end a paean to her grief, the grief of a goddess who is vulnerable to that most mortal of emotions.

Lucrece is in a way the counterpart, a strong woman wronged despite her strength. It is a rape story, an intimate "me too" story, articulating her torment. Her lines, mostly internal monologue, are two-thirds of the poem. She reasons with Tarquin in the same way that the Countess of Salisbury reasoned with King Edward, but fruitlessly.

Tarquin has more depth than most of my male characters to that point; he struggles within himself to justify his actions, knowing that he is in the wrong. Although he has a conscience that speaks to him, he feels compelled to dismiss it stubbornly.

Feminists today might see Lucrece as a stereotype of women who define themselves as sexual objects. It might seem unliberated for her to regard her chastity as a treasure, and to commit suicide at the loss of that purity at the centre of herself, in essence capitulating to male dominance. I would disagree. I meant her valuation of self as an assertion, a direct action, not a mistaken displacement of self. She is not a possession of either her husband or her rapist; she is in possession of her final exit. We don't condemn Juliet for her suicide, do we? In both cases, something has been disrupted, shattered; is it only love that justifies suicide? Just sayin', don't be harsh now on my Lucrece.

Those two narrative poems gave me a break from the demands of the stage. The break confirmed for me that gender would be an essential aspect of my work going forward, not just a sub-current beneath the surface.

King James 1 ascended ten years later in the plague year of 1603 and, without any sense of the irony of abandoning his post, immediately went on Progress, to avoid the pestiferous environs of London. His first stop was Wilton, where I made sure he saw a performance of *Much Ado About Nothing* on 2 December. I made my choice of plays as a deliberate counter-move after he had arrested my friend Sir Walter Raleigh. James had heard that Walter was a spy. The message of *Much Ado* is that hearsay is insufficient grounds for judgement.

In the play, Count Claudio falls in love with Hero, but then believes a malicious lie about her. She collapses when he confronts her, and she is presumed dead, but later she revives and is proven innocent in the end. The performance had an immediate but incomplete effect. James spared Walter's life, though he kept him in prison for a decade before releasing him to make a voyage in search of Spanish gold. James was an unfeeling beast, a weak man who was paranoid about his potential enemies, and a cold misogynist to boot. He feared witchcraft above all.

I used all my female witchery to convince him I was nothing more than a society lady, not a threat. He was susceptible to flattery, and to luxury. He praised the setting and accommodations at Wilton, which he had never seen until that visit.

Much Ado shows one strain of my writing: I often had a purpose and a targeted audience in mind. I liked to sway peoples' opinions with subtlety, giving them room to draw their own conclusions, unaware that I had planted the seeds of their thinking.

Would a man even have titled a play about infidelity much ado about nothing? Read between the lines, please, to see a woman's perspective, my perspective. To a man, an accusation of infidelity sows seeds of growing uncertainty, even after being disproved. To a woman, it's more precipitous: he's guilty or not guilty, and then decide whether to move on.

Other plays I wrote with James in mind were *Measure for Measure, Lear,* and *Macbeth,* all of these about failures of leadership. *Antony and Cleopatra* was written then as well, to give James a wider sense of the strength a woman is capable of.

All right, this is what some of you might have been waiting for. What did I really have in mind when I wrote all those plays about women accused of infidelity?

One strong thread is rumour, a topic that also fascinated the classical poets. Four of my best plays are about false accusations against women: *Much Ado, The Winter's Tale, Othello,* and *Hamlet.* I was accustomed to the devastation that rumours could have, and also with the possibility that some rumours are true. But plays are about actions, and the men who believe rumours or act upon hasty assumptions are likely to be catastrophically wrong.

Hamlet's assumption was that his mother had a hand in his father's death. In my play, I left that as an unknown but in my own mind Gertrude was not aware that her husband had been poisoned.

Hamlet's uncertainty was more than a knee-jerk male response, however. It was central to his being, and to his humanity. Uncertainty is one of the aspects of human nature that preoccupied me in the later works of my career.

*

It was a challenge living under the reign of James 1, a reprobate who was definitely a douchepizzle. (Isn't it wonderful how very popular slams have become in the modern age? How I might throw them out now!) But I understood the court and knew how to manoeuvre around the threat of disfavour and imprisonment. Mostly, James needed flattery. I gave him that in the play *Macbeth*, reassuring him that kings and their heirs were inviolable. That play took for granted that pretenders to the throne were likely to be led by witches and unsexed wives, and would in the end be beheaded. James was happy with that scenario; he especially liked the long line of kings projected as the heirs of the legitimate king.

34.   THE MALE PSYCHE

Returning to London after the interruption for the plagues, and having delved more deeply into the interior lives of two male characters, the shallow Adonis and the tormented Tarquin in my narrative poems, I had in mind to portray men, my second favourite subject, with more substance. I sought to stretch my art to make them less flat. Still, at this stage the men mostly occupied narrow roles. I became interested in the ways that gender was an aspect of power. Being born to power does not convey leadership; being born outside power allows constricted avenues to acquisition of power.

RICHARD 2

In the backstory of the Henry plays the banished Henry Bolingbroke returns to England, gathers an army, and assumes the crown as Henry 4. He deposes Richard, imprisons him and has him murdered. My portrayal of Richard shows him as a King who is was forced to look inside himself and find the basis for the potential nobility he has not shown before the moment he is in prison.

Richard is most a leader when he is losing his crown. The capital supporting his status, however, is mostly on loan from his country, which puts leaders in a position of strength and then awaits the outcome. Richard himself was never strong except that his place was one of ultimate power. Too late, he realizes the weight of that position. In contrast, Henry 4 quickly ascertained what it meant to be King, and his son Hal learned that decisiveness as well.

It is not just kings who need to learn the strengths and weaknesses inside them. My next several plays depict other strata: a woman who leans forward to seize her power potential; male intellectuals who find themselves lacking but have the grace to concede their faults; and a common tradesman who has a glimpse of the human potential to brush against divinity.

MERCHANT OF VENICE: SHYLOCK

It's what's inside a character that allows full portraiture. Like Richard 2, Shylock in *Merchant of Venice* has an interior life. Shylock was my most full male portrait thus far. He is driven by narrow vices, but he also reveals the pain of being an outsider. He gives us a taste of the major roles to come in my later plays, where unsympathetic characters nevertheless rise to heights, or sink to depths of internal passion.

Unfortunately, Shylock's engine is one of revenge. Given the option of showing mercy, he can only nurse his own injuries. Although Shylock's conversion at the end of the play is forced, in that regard it is similar to many other plays where characters do not willingly come to new versions of themselves. The possibility of conversion rests on a person discovering an inner character quite different from the outer one.

What's inside will out. The caskets prove it, Shylock's conversion demonstrates its necessity, and the resolution at the end declares it. Character will arise from the detritus of life's disappointments—the good has the strength to supplant the bad—at least it is so in the idealized world of comedy. In *The Comical History of the Merchant of Venice*, we see flawed characters redeemed severally. The conversion pattern that had begun with the very first plays underlies this one throughout, including servants finding better masters.

COMEDY OF ERRORS

I found relief from the questions of cosmic judgement when I worked on comedies after the plague. *Comedy of Errors* is the farcical story of two sets of identical twins. The action includes wrongful beatings, seduction, and false accusations. It has a bit more variety of male portraits, but they are woodcuts: one of blind justice, one of vain materialism, and one of ethical probity. The errors are both male and female, but the only character with any depth is the injured wife, Adriana. She tries to make the best of the difficult challenge of meeting the double standards of her community in Ephesus. She makes a speech much like that of the Countess in *Edward 3*, reminding her husband of the integrity and sacredness of marriage vows. The men are comic figures, while she rises up in full, conflicted vulnerability. Once again, however, I kept falling just short of gender equity. I could well portray fascinating women, but the men continued to be almost all boring.

SETTING

A note about setting: what difference does it make to set a play outside of England? Almost all of my plays are set in foreign lands. Among the dozen in England, most are history plays; *Cymbaline* and *Lear* are set in a mythic England, and *Merry Wives* has its location in England merely to suit the character Falstaff.

My fascination began with *Titus* and the spirit of revenge as a facet of Roman times. In *Comedy of Errors*, I portrayed a huge difference between the materialistic spirit of Syracuse in Sicily, and the more generous spirit of Ephesus in Turkey. Are those characterizations very accurate? Hardly.

I confess to not being capable of deep analysis of the temper of foreign peoples, but it worked well on stage to set up some bald contrasts with England. The rigidities of noble families and court influence in England would have complicated any play set in England. Settings in foreign lands allowed me more latitude in weighing the local thumb on the scales.

LOVE'S LABOUR'S LOST

I had two reasons for allowing this to be the first published play with the name WS as author, subtle reasons that undercut his authorship. First, the play is based on a French play (Primaudaye's *French Academy*), and WS did not read or speak French. Second, some parts of it derived from my brother Philip's work, staking a claim in a way for my authorship.

It was great fun to portray a group of men in *Love's Labour's Lost* taking themselves very seriously, debating how to pursue a pure intellectual life, i.e. without women.

With all due respect to my life-long friend Sir Francis Bacon, the world of ideas engages the mind wonderfully; but ideas rarely dictate events and the events are not directly under the control of the brilliant thinkers.

The King of Navarre and three friends abjure the company of women to focus on their studies. They are comic, but at least they have many interesting layers of foolishness mixed with their earnest ambitions. After many long speeches about the beauty of an intellectual life, they cannot resist wooing women once the entourage of the Queen of France arrives.

The women are again much more clever, more aware than the men, besting them at their own game of masking: "there's no such sport as sport o'er thrown." In the end, the men are hoisted by their own petard, when the Queen gives them the ultimatum that she will not accept a marriage proposal until its sincerity has been demonstrated by a year of "forlorn and naked hermitage remote from all the pleasures of the world." Their wooing words are put to the test. The ending, once again, remains ambiguous.

Men do tend to believe in their own words, and in their schemes, and in their pretensions. In that regard, I felt that I pierced the male psyche to the heart. But comedies with the men as the butt of the joke did not satisfy my desire to portray men at their best.

*

Wanting to understand men even better in the years after 1593, I wrote *1 & 2 Henry IV, Henry V, Much Ado About Nothing, Julius Caesar, As You Like It, The Merry Wives of Windsor,* and *Twelfth Night.* Men began to take shape in the best lights possible, most notably in *Henry V*. These were all character-driven plays, showcasing both men and women in leading roles, probing the intricacies of male-female relations, with its many sparks and its variable outcomes.

Relationships between sexes had been a live issue in the earlier plays, but in the later plays I realized that the bonds between men are often just as strong as their bonds with women, even as the relationships between sexes continue to sway the plots.

What does it mean to be a man? I had such good examples growing up, in my father, my uncle Leicester, my brother, and my husband. I plead guilty to seeing men as leaders in their best capacities, with women in support and in shared guardianship as their partners in a sexist world. Things were changing, but the assumption remained that men were expected to step forward, and their paths were open; women could step forward, but their paths were obstructed. Still are; but back then, it was deeply structural. Women were not allowed to speak in law courts, for instance, and that's why Portia had to dress as a man to argue the case against Shylock. It was difficult to portray men and women as equals. That was never quite my goal. But I still yearned to capture a man at his best.

A MIDSUMMER NIGHT'S DREAM

With Philip in mind, and the Arcadian ideal, I turned to Roman myth. *A Midsummer Night's Dream* was a way for me to remind myself of Philip.

Moreover, I had an idea that I could give two of the men in the story more depth.

When Bottom awakes from his dream, his enforced conversion shows him the possibility of something other than ordinary life, an awareness of another dimension of beauty and nobility. "The eye of man hath not heard, the ear of man hath not seen, man's hand is not able to taste, his tongue to conceive, nor his heart to report what my dream was."

Bottom combines male bombast with poetic tenderness. The lesson there is that a man must see himself as an ass before he can rise above his lower instincts.

And I could redeem Duke Theseus, conqueror of the Amazons, from his initial misogyny by allowing him a display of wisdom at the end. He shows a perspective much wider than his position of power. He had won his bride through military action but I could give him a broader understanding of the dynamics of gender interaction.

First, he is gracious to the lovers and then overrules Egeus's continued assertion of parental rights over his daughter Hermia. Second, he is gracious to the players, encouraging the court to accept the labourers/actors for what they are, "for never anything can be amiss when simpleness and duty tender it." His values are as noble as any other characters in the other plays.

And third, he understands poets, though somewhat tongue in cheek. I was poking fun at myself when I gave him these lines:

> "The poet's eye, in fine frenzy rolling,
> Doth glance from heaven to earth, from earth to heaven;
> And as imagination bodies forth
> The forms of things unknown, the poet's pen
> Turns them to shapes and gives to airy nothing
> A local habitation and a name.
> Such tricks hath strong imagination
> That if it would but apprehend some joy,
> It comprehends some bringer of that joy;
> Or in the night, imagining some fear,
> How easy is a bush supposed a bear.

But most of all for me *Midsummer* has aspects that speak to my family's preoccupation with the pastoral. What might be a sort of Arcadian ideal? The very thing we see in *A Midsummer Night's Dream*: a ruler laying down his arms, governing a society that accepts and supports all levels, and enjoying the pleasures of a life of leisure. Alas, a dream is not the real world I most fervently wanted to portray.

HENRY 5

The apotheosis of what it means to be a man is shown in *Henry 5*, which enacts events leading up to the battle of Agincourt, where young King Henry shows his leadership. From his early years, Hal had cultivated broad connections with commoners and adventurer soldiers; as a young prince and then King, he has more weighty responsibilities. Men show the best of leadership qualities and the best of themselves when they take on serious business. Good leaders combine ambition with compassion. The speeches of the mature Henry express his heart's truest intent with subtlety, wisdom, and compassion.

What can ennoble a man? The answer is that at his best a good man knows when and how to take responsibility. It is inherently sexist, but for those times and somewhat still today, taking responsibility is a version of the best self of any man, and indeed any person. In the history plays when men take charge, their best traits are a true sense of honour, including penitence for the inherited wrongs that gave them their positions, and good judgement to go along with the power and status that a man inherits by gender. Henry 5 knows when to execute traitors and looters, when to spare the conquered town, and when to forgive the small offences of the rough Welshman and the muttering soldier. He also has an acute awareness of the limbs and heads and families that are at stake in the battles he undertakes. He even has a willingness to face his detractors if he fails, and he has a recognition that there could be higher powers behind fortunate humans. Henry fulfills all possible expectations. Fashioning a man at his best gave me a thrill that had been absent in all the earlier plays.

Unfortunately, that side of men is rare. Mostly, power is sought for its own sake, or is based on the mistaken perceptions that others are threats. Always, these are attempts to control the uncontrollable. Many of my plays were cautionary tales about the male fixation on being in control: *Othello*, *Macbeth*, *Hamlet*, and all the history plays except the *H4* and *H5* history plays. Kings hold wide sway, but the best leaders, male or female, know that control is beyond any royal command. There is a transaction to work out between conception and success.

MERCHANT OF VENICE: Portia

Undeniably, Portia is the true hero of *Merchant*. She commands the action and the stage the way Henry V will command his domain. Granted, hers is a domain with constraints and in that sense only somewhat better than the times it comes from. As she says herself, "the lottery of my destiny / Bars me the right of voluntary choosing" (II.i.4-5). Nevertheless, Portia stands alone as an Elizabethan woman who can succeed in the legal world; there wasn't anything else like it within England. A woman was only tolerated "professionally" for testimonies at the Inns of Court, meaning as prostitute or domestic servant. I am thrilled that things have continued to change, incrementally. Shout out to RBG.

Portia has a capacity for independent thought and action. She inserts herself into decisive moments, preserves integrity despite constraints which limit choices, and has an indomitable, gritty spirit of self-determination, tied to a fierce commitment to the close connections of heart and home. She has precise knowledge of her wealth, and acts decisively to use it to seek resolution of Bassanio's needs and Shylock's demands. She is at least equal in mercantile standing to any of the merchants in the play.

Like Juliet in *Romeo and Juliet*, Portia knows the value of a contract: Juliet enforces a definite appointment to meet Friar Laurence; similarly, Portia exchanges rings as a symbol of their bond, letting Bassanio know immediately that he must accept responsibilities when he takes her hand as partner. Whenever resolutions are sought or found or even constrained within a hierarchy, the spirit is one of negotiation. Portia's generous speech immediately after Bassanio wins her hand flatters him with what might sound like a concession, but it has conditions to it, and she manages these conditions with a clear head.

I was not what people nowadays would call a feminist. I deferred to male dominance as a *sine non qua*. Overturning the *status quo* was unthinkable but confronting it was exquisitely satisfying.

I titled this play as a *Comical History* because it has the foundation of all comedy, an idealistic hope for resolution of differences. One aspect of the ideal world conjured at times in the play is that mercy has absolute value aside from any issue of the calculations of justice, sometimes without even an expectation of repentance. Antonio offers a tainted form of mercy requiring Shylock to convert and to bequeath his wealth upon his disloyal daughter; but Portia's famous speech goes further, articulating this sense of the value of mercy in more generalized terms:

> The quality of mercy is not strained.
> It droppeth as the gentle rain from heaven
> Upon the place beneath. It is twice blest:
> It blesseth him that gives, and him that takes.
> 'Tis mightiest in the mightiest; it becomes
> The thronèd monarch better than his crown.
> His sceptre shows the force of temporal power,
> The attribute to awe and majesty,
> Wherein doth sit the dread and fear of kings;
> But mercy is above this sceptred sway.
> It is enthronèd in the hearts of kings;
> It is an attribute to God himself;
> And earthly power doth then show likest God's
> When mercy seasons justice. Therefore, Jew,
> Though justice be thy plea, consider this:
> That in the course of justice none of us
> Should see salvation. We do pray for mercy,
> And that same prayer doth teach us all to render
> The deeds of mercy.

Yes, there is a bias in favour of Christianity in my plays, but not in a sectarian or dogmatic way. As Desmond Tutu suggested, a path to truth and reconciliation has existed ever since Christians championed the course of forgiveness. Under God, who stands unblemished? And bear in mind also that my emphasis on mercy presents the best side of Christianity. I certainly knew the more damaging sides of sectarianism as well.

*

TROILUS AND CRESSIDA

Troilus and Cressida are all too human, aspiring to the heights of love without any sense of how to make it work. During the Trojan War, the Trojan prince Troilus falls in love with Cressida and marries her. What drives Troilus and Cressida apart is that they lack a clear sense of what love means. In youth, appearance seems all, and the woman is a prize to be won. He speaks only of appearance, "her eyes, her hair, her cheek, her gait, her voice…, a treasure," while she speaks of herself as a prize he must earn. He refers to her twice as his "achievement." He seeks the security of a marriage bond because, in a time of war, he cannot be patient for this new relationship to sort through any uncertainties.

In a deal made by the Trojan generals, Cressida is traded on the morning after their wedding night to the Greeks for a Trojan prisoner. Her father, whose sympathies lie with the Greeks, is unaware of their marriage, and assents to the trade. The assumption is that she will be treated honourably, and she is.

However, Cressida, crest-fallen, now trusting no one, betrays Troilus immediately in the Greek camp, flirting with the Greek prince Diomedes. She discovers that she doesn't have any bond at all when she becomes a hostage to the Greek forces. It is the obverse of Romeo and Juliet; there doesn't seem to be anything solid inside these pandered lovers—they do not prove true. Their love depends on the circumstances.

In the changed circumstance, Troilus becomes a better citizen. Troilus sees her across the battlements flirting with Greek soldiers and his consequent hatred of the Greeks makes him a more determined warrior. Stimulus and response.

Pandarus has the easy, greasy role but the outcome is neither the fault of the lovers nor of Pandarus; it is a condition of the ancient world, where mortal endeavours depend in part on the smiles and frowns of the gods. Pandarus is neither evil nor cynical; he sees love as a conquest with a possibly pleasant outcome. He is Puck: "the man shall have his mare again." When relationships are casual, and people do not feel responsible for their own fates, their emotions become as unpredictable as the winds of war. The outcome is often catastrophic.

Here is Cressida, thinking to herself as she is wooed by her new Greek suitor:

> Troilus, farewell. One eye yet looks on thee
> But with my heart the other eye doth see.
> Ah, poor our sex! This fault in us I find,
> The error of our eye directs our mind:
> What error leads must err. O, then conclude:
> Minds swayed by eyes are full of turpitude.

This is a reverse twist on Helena's words in *MND*, "Love looks not with the eyes, but with the mind; and therefore is wing'd Cupid painted blind." Helena is mistaken, of course, because love does look with the eyes. Cressida is right that "the error of our eye directs our mind." Will Helena's marriage last longer than Cressida's? Maybe not.

What is true love, anyway? Hamlet and Othello think they have it; they are men who truly, deeply, madly believe in the love they proclaim, but self-belief defines its own boundaries. Outside those boundaries lies the land of doubt. Misprision is the norm. The bitter truth is that men and women are rather prone to disharmony. Even in comedies, marriage only resolves the conflicts of the moment.

But love is not only between the sexes. It is also between people of the same sex. I am not talking about homosexuality here, an issue that belonged in private bedrooms until the great writers Whitman, Colette and Wilde broke down the door. I am talking about the magnetic power of friendship.

*

The bonds between men and women often fray, but I had seen in my own life that the bonds between men, and between women, are often stronger. Those bonds last even after severe tests of their strength. For men, the strongest relationships seem cemented with other men, and the same goes for bonds between women.

The strongest sympathies lie between persons of the same sex: Helena and Hermia, who grew up together in *Midsummer*; Rosalind and Celia in *As You Like It*; the Merry Wives who trick Falstaff; Emelia and Desdemona in Othello; Helena and the Countess in *All's Well*; and even Gertrude bringing flowers to eulogize Ophelia. Gertrude touchingly honours Ophelia while Hamlet self-pityingly leaps into her grave! Gertrude speaks more clearly from her heart than Hamlet does.

JULIUS CAESAR

The spirit of male connection dominates the Henry plays, particularly between Falstaff and Hal, and Hotspur and Hal in *Henry 4*. Male bonds prevail there, and are also especially strong in *Romeo & Juliet, Othello, The Two Noble Kinsmen*, and many of the history plays. But the best example is *Julius Caesar*.

This is a play about loyalty between friends. Brutus is Caesar's friend and still claims to be so after he stabs him. Octavius at the end praises Brutus as the noblest Roman of them all—even insurrection can be forgiven if honour holds. Antony on the other hand is not a true mate; he speaks eloquently as a friend, only as a cover for ambition.

In *Julius Caesar*, women have only 4.5% of the lines, and their influence is overtly dismissed, but the affections which are usually assumed to be female territory are embodied in male friendships such as that between Cassius and Brutus. Those two have a nearly fatal argument but reconnect in the end. Bonds between brothers overcome all disagreements.

> CASSIUS. Have you not love enough to bear with me,
> When that rash humor which my mother gave me
> Makes me forgetful?
>
> BRUTUS. Yes, Cassius, and from henceforth,
> When you are over-earnest with your Brutus,
> He'll think your mother chides, and leave you so.

In other words, they believe women are emotional, men stoic, but beneath their stoicism is a riptide of belief in friendship. It is what is inside that drives them, more than the politics.

*

MEASURE FOR MEASURE

In *Measure for Measure*, the Duke leaves Angelo in charge of Vienna to curb the immorality of the city. Although Angelo is a harsh administrator of justice, he lusts for the nun Isabella and uses coercion to get her agree to sleep with him. By a bed trick, she gets Angelo to sleep with his fiancé instead. In the end, Angelo's punishment is to be married against his will to his fiancé. The character Lucio suffers a similar punishment.

What works well on stage is that forced marriages are a hoot. But do the marriages make the women beneficiaries, or sacrificial lambs? In this case, the resolution has complexities that reflect human uncertainties; but in the full context, the matches are made to order for the women. Angelo and Lucio are brought to heel by their marriages. Mariana is in love with Angelo and marriage is the only proper course. Lucio's wife Juliet has no spoken lines at all but again, Lucio is her only proper option. The grey areas of these decisions provide a beautiful *chiaroscuro* to the main plot. Still, these are characters in a very broken world.

Isabella, the main character, has the most subtle resolution. In the concluding scene the Duke asks Isabella to leave the convent and marry him, but she does not give him a single word in answer during that scene. The play leaves the audience with the pleasant prospect of an advantageous marriage, without the sense that she has given her full assent. Isabella leaves the stage with the Duke, perhaps hand in hand. Can she accept this dictated resolution as one made for her? I think so, just as much as any woman who receives a marriage offer she cannot see to refuse. Arranged and enforced marriages can sometimes be to the advantage of women who are not in a position to command.

What is going on inside these women? Their honour accepts only one resolution: a respectable marriage. Isabella is no fool. She manoeuvres herself around some dangerous situations without losing her control. She never once compromises her integrity. She will decide on her own terms, surely.

Look at the whole play in terms of mercy, the decision to see people's faults in the best light. Isabella might choose the Duke with his own imperfections, rather than continue to stay in a convent protected from the vagaries of human nature. Ask John Milton what he thought of this play; his *Aereopagitica* reflects his understanding that a protected virtue is no virtue at all. Nevertheless, the unanswered proposition means that tensions linger. She is a bit like Kate in *Taming*, retaining a form of control even when silent.

ALL'S WELL THAT ENDS WELL

The next play I wrote, *All's Well That Ends Well*, also has characters married against their will. In this case, Helena has the power of her choice for a spouse, in reward for curing the King of France of a fistula (a boil) that made him impotent and unable to stand (pun intended). Her choice, Bertram, disdains her for her lack of breeding: she is merely a physician's daughter with no title in her family, an orphan under the care of Bertram's mother. The King, grateful for his cure, says he can easily confer a title upon Helena so the question should be her merit; consequently, Bertram accedes but only under royal instruction. Before consummating the marriage, however, Bertram leaves for war. After the war, he consummates the marriage only by a bed trick arranged by Helena: he thinks he is sleeping with a woman he met on his military jaunt to Italy. It takes much doing to allow a woman to choose, but in this case, Helen had me pulling the strings.

After *Measure*, this is the second play in sequence where men are wedded under duress. In earlier plays such as *R&J* and *MND*, forced marriages are abhored, but in this comedy, Bertram accepts Helena's love in the final scene and reciprocates in accepting marriage, keeping his word as he had promised in his parting letter to Helena that he would honour the marriage if she ever bedded him and bore their child. Moreover, another woman, Diana, a poor widow's daughter who assisted Helena's plot, is told by the King to choose *her* own husband, with a dowry at the King's expense!

Two women are given their choice with no suggestion that it will lead to bad marriages. In the end a valid marriage is in itself a solid foundation; and if at first the partner might be unwilling, affection might come later. It is no worse than the advice many parents have given to reluctant newlyweds.

Helena's love is entire; she declares her love early in a speech to Bertram's mother, *before* she has received the Duke's dispensation to choose her own husband, saying that she cannot help her affection, it "riddle-like lives sweetly" within her, without any expectation of fulfillment. She accepts a husband who disdained her because her love is strong enough to prevail. She adds love to the equation.

We have to sympathize with her, but in the context of other women who love strongly without prevailing, the picture is again of the sense within all the plays that the tensions between sexes linger. That they do, *nicht wahr?* Nevertheless, Helena's choice reigns, and that is a triumph.

37.   LATE PLAYS

Histories and comedies share a tendency toward an ending that celebrates the possiblities of the future. In the final stage of my career, I preferred more definite endings depicting the cataclysmic rifts that tear men and women apart, such as political faction, betrayal, disloyalty, jealousy, ambition, materialism, and the mechanisms of justice. These are bitter truths because they suggest that in the end all alliances and relationships are circumstantial.

Men and women might seek love but they cannot ignore the context of politics and factions. I would not be a good matchmaker; I see the problems lurking behind all connections.

Mostly, people in power make one fatal assumption, that neither they nor others have any choice but to make commands. Their relationships with loved ones and collaborators and servants seem to them to be fixed, but their connections are transient. Vulnerability sits uneasily on the heads of power.

What is the final message of my plays? That attempts to control life have tragic consequences. Control aims at a clear purpose, but the consequences will usually be unintended. Those who attempt control are generally male, to no one's surprise, but it is a failing of both genders. Always, these failings are richly generated, from the most human of traits, not destructive or selfish ones, but from a belief in the ideal values that made them great leaders, though flawed.

Recognition that control has been lost, as in the case of Lear, can lead to bitterness. Grief, is there anything else more powerful? Yes, I was to discover, in my probing of the internal lives of characters: grief mingled with regret, with guilt, with musings over mistakings. Grief arising from the awareness that one has caused one's own downfall. My early work had more trust in hope, in the power of resolution. My later work recognized the kind of grief that makes the end of life or the anticipation of the afterlife a living hell.

My late plays make an abrupt turn toward a bitter, unvarnished assessment of the false values of the world. The endings of *Hamlet, Othello, Lear,* and *Timon* grow progressively bleak. These are warnings in apocalyptic words, with king, warrior, and merchant exposed as bankrupts. It is revolutionary stuff.

KING LEAR

The magnificent thundering of its title character dominates *King Lear*, of course. But what is he thundering about? Once again, tensions erupt between the sexes, especially between father and daughters. Lear assumes that his daughters' love for him can be relied upon as a natural process; in reality, familial bonds do not preclude tensions, no matter how much one lover believes the love is sacred. Cordelia also believes the bond is sacred, but she leaves it unspoken, another among many female characters whose silence drives the dynamic. I consider my public silence as true to the norm.

In contrast to Cordelia, her sisters Regan and Goneril express love but destroy their own familial foundation by slighting their duties to their father and casting him out into the wilderness. As Lear says, "how sharper than a serpent's tooth it is to have a thankless child." Bereft, Lear wanders about in a thunderstorm, howling "blow wind and crack your cheeks," a phrasing that will surface again in *Macbeth*. But to Lear the physical storm is completely dwarfed by comparison to the "greater malady" of his daughters' filial ingratitude causing the "tempest in [his] mind." The turmoil in nature is an image of the rift in the family. Soon enough, the sisters' lack of a sense of familial ties leads to a division between the sisters themselves, and in that division the powers of France see the opportunity for an invasion. The disruption of the natural order has spread from family to nature to country.

Once he sees that he must accept his disappointment in family, Lear takes the philosophical angle suitable to playwrights, and to all writers:

> No, no. Come, let's away to prison:
> We two alone will sing like birds i' th' cage.
> When thou dost ask me blessing, I'll kneel down
> And ask of thee forgiveness: So we'll live,
> And pray, and sing, and tell old tales, and laugh
> At gilded butterflies, and hear poor rogues

Talk of court news; and we'll talk with them too—
Who loses and who wins, who's in, who's out—
And take upon's the mystery of things,
As if we were God's spies: and we'll wear out,
In a walled prison, packs and sects of great ones,
That ebb and flow by the moon.

No better epitaph for a poet, than to have been one of God's spies, and to exult in that role, even at the lowest moment. Lear has an exquisite sense of loss, reminiscent of Richard 2 who only knew the value of his crown when he had lost it. Lear rises from that sense of loss to a superior height, looking down upon the poor slaves who continue to tilt at Fortune. But fortune knocks him with grief and regret in one final blow, the death of his dear Cordelia. His final recognition is that of Oedipus, a more fitting parallel here than in *Hamlet*. Lear is at his Colonus, no going back, except inward toward self-knowledge, a journey worth the sharing.

TIMON OF ATHENS

Greece has the reputation of being the cradle of democracy, but it could only do so as a wealthy nation dependent upon enforced slavery. Beneath the veneer of prosperous civility, there is a celebration of military might that undermines the harmony of the nation. I meant this play as a warning to England; I like to think that history shows that I have pointed England in the right direction, toward prosperity shared, and military might only when threatened.

The wealthy and popular Timon ignores warnings that his extravagance will exhaust his fortune. When he eventually becomes penniless, he loses all the friends money bought him, and leaves Athens to live in a cave. There, he discovers gold and funds a war against Athens. He dies a traitor. Even his mother disowns him.

Timon of Athens is *Macbeth* without the witches and without the Lady. Timon cannot seek compromise, only confrontation. It is a masculine world without the necessary counterbalance of feminine virtues. I must admit it was satisfying to portray his mother rejecting him. I had been tempted in similar moments in my own life. My two venal and small-minded sons were never military conquerors, but they were antithetical to my own sense of right and wrong. Even a mother can have her limits of empathy, her surfeit of excuses.

Unlike Lear, Timon never comes to a lonely recognition of his own failing. Instead, he becomes bitter, and blames society. As thieves are about to rob him of gold he dug from the ground in the wilderness, Timon expresses the sense of the wasteland apparent in so many late plays:

> The sun's a thief, and with his great attraction
> Robs the vast sea. The moon's an arrant thief,
> And her pale fire she snatches from the sun.
> The sea's a thief, whose liquid surge resolves
> The moon into salt tears. The earth's a thief,
> That feeds and breeds by a composture stol'n
> From gen'ral excrement. Each thing's a thief:
> The laws, your curb and whip, in their rough power
> Have uncheque'd theft. Love not yourselves. Away,
> Rob one another. There's more gold. Cut throats;
> All that you meet are thieves. To Athens go,
> Break open shops; nothing can you steal
> But thieves do lose it: steal no less for this I give you,
> And gold confound you howsoe'er! Amen.

Set this accusatory sonnet by Timon in contrast to the harmony of the spheres at the end of *Merchant*, to appreciate the change in tone of these later plays. Timon had been under the illusion that he was in control of his city, but now he blames greed for dooming not only him, but also the common good, to failure. He has turned into an anarchist. Only compromise could have saved him.

It is ironic that he blames greed, since his extravagance caused his downfall in the first place. And it is ironic that he rejects compromise, since the entire ethic of Athens was to come to common consensus. Timon's combative demons lived inside him along with the angels that could have saved him. His demise fits Aristotle's notion of tragedy, with no recognition of his flaws to redeem him.

*

When WS left the theatre world in London, my career also came to an end. I wrote a play for the occasion, about myself, not WS, about my career winding down.

Prospero, the usurped Duke of Milan, stranded on an island and commanding the elements through magic, causes the shipwreck of his evil brother, but sparing his life. After teaching his brother some life lessons, Prospero then reclaims his title and returns to his Dukedom.

The Tempest announces my departure from the theatre world, my shedding of the cloak of magical concoction. It is, in other words, completely me. It has all my major themes, including vain attempts at control, the perils of love and family, the brute division of the sexes, and the power of imagination, but especially mercy. Prospero says at the very beginning that he will choose repentance over punishment for his brother and his conspirators, the "they" in the following lines:

> Though with their high wrongs I am struck to th' quick,
> Yet, with my nobler reason, 'gainst my fury
> Do I take part. The rarer action is
> In virtue than in vengeance. They being penitent,
> The sole drift of my purpose doth extend
> Not a frown further

In the end mercy prevails, even for the most rebellious and scheming of the lot. And in the epilogue Prospero also asks for mercy, submitting himself and his play to the judgement of the audience:

> … my ending is despair,
> Unless I be reliev'd by prayer,
> Which pierces so, that it assaults
> Mercy itself, and frees all faults.
> As you from crimes would pardon'd be,
> Let your indulgence set me free.

The image of prayer assaulting the prison bars of despair brings us back to the word "resolve." Prospero has resolved the conflicts within the story, but it is up to the audience to decide whether his resolution succeeds. He cannot sit upon his own judgement. He asks the audience to accept the core truth of a story graced by reconciliation. Prayer here takes the form of applause, meaning the good wishes of the audience. He empowers the audience to endorse the story that has been told, giving it the power to "Free all faults." Prospero stands as patriarch here but he sounds feminine tunes, specifically of forgiveness, acceptance and inclusion. It is a magnanimous farewell, and it serves as mine as well, merely asking the audiences over the ages to applaud if they will.

*

What does it mean to be human? Caliban has all the elements, including a keen perception of music, an innate sense of the harmony of the physical world, a susceptibility to being deceived by outer appearances and muddled by liquor, and most of all, a tendency toward sin. It might seem strange to see the play as a portrait of what it means to be human, with the plot's heavy layers of witches, fairies, and mythological beings, but really, it is my final statement on human nature, including its spiritual side. That which is human is always what makes for great drama. I just loved keeping my eyes open for all that humanity going on around me. I was an observer, a learner, not a wizard.

*

A key thread in the play, consistent with the body of my work as a whole, is that of families. Five characters demonstrate the importance of family: Prospero in his care for his daughter, Ferdinand in his labouring to earn the hand of Miranda, Alonso in his grieving for the son he thinks he has lost, Antonio in his original betrayal of his brother Prospero, and Caliban in his inherited "darkness" from his mother Sycorax—all attest to the primacy of family. Add to that the dynastic marriage that seals the restoration of peace between Milan and Naples.

*

And once again, loss is at the heart of the transformations that take place in *The Tempest*. Both Caliban and Prospero grieve over what they had lost, and Alonso grieves for his son. Those losses give them the capacity to see what matters to them, and to change for the sake of what they now realise they really need to honour.

*

So too with my own sharpest loss, that of my brilliant brother Philip, more searing than the loss of other siblings, of my parents, and even of my own child. I cannot tell you the thing itself; every substance of a grief has twenty shadows, each with a life of its own. Philip was the noblest of us all in the Elizabethan era. His death became my own work's underpinning.

Everything I wrote had behind it my memory of him, every *Psalm* translation, every sonnet, and every play. My sixty years, two-thirds of them as a writer, taught me one lesson above all: that the regal coronet of *any* writing life is the iron band of sorrow. Decorative images and fanciful designs are mere caps worn for amusement. In the arts, death and grief grip their corporeal forms in the spaces beyond the joys of life.

Loss underlies many of the greatest of works. The power of *Oedipus Rex* leads inevitably to the even more intense tragedy of *Antigone* and on to the cathartic release of *Oedipus at Colonus*. Why did Dante need Beatrice as Muse of *The Divine Comedy*? Milton wrote of loss of Paradise, but his elegy *Lycidas* might stand as his greatest work. The truest measure of any *corpus* is the distress of loss, regret, or grief. Charlie Chaplin's Little Tramp and Robin Williams' conflicted characters would agree. Even the movie *Beelzebub* explores grief, as does *Peter Pan*.

*

TWO GENTLEMEN REVISITED: *TWO NOBLE KINSMEN*

My very last play was a collaboration with Fletcher; the story goes back to Boccacio and the genius Chaucer. The parts I wrote enhanced the female characters. The play also makes use of my own experience growing up.

Emilia has this to say to Theseus's wife Hippolyta about friendship: that female friendship might be even stronger than that between a man and a woman.

> EMILIA. ...I was acquainted
> Once with a time when I enjoyed a playfellow
> ...when our count was each eleven.
> HIPPOLYTA. 'Twas Flavina.
> EMILIA. Yes.
> You talk of Pirithous' and Theseus' love:
> Theirs has more ground, is more maturely seasoned,
> More buckled with strong judgement, and their needs
> The one of th'other may be said to water
> Their intertangled roots of love; but I

And she I sigh and spoke of were things innocent,
Loved for we did, and like the elements,
That know not what, nor why, yet do effect
Rare issues by their operance, our souls
Did so to one another. What she liked
Was then of me approved; what not, condemned—
No more arraignment. The flower that I would pluck
And put between my breasts—O then but beginning
To swell about the blossom—she would long
Till she had such another, and commit it
To the like innocent cradle, where, phoenix-like,
They died in perfume. On my head no toy
But was her pattern. Her affections—pretty,
Though happily her careless wear—I followed
For my most serious decking. Had mine ear
Stol'n some new air, or at adventure hummed one,
From musical coinage, why, it was a note
Whereon her spirits would sojourn—rather dwell on—
And sing it in her slumbers. This rehearsal—
Which seely innocence wots well, comes in
Like old emportment's bastard—has this end:
That the true love 'tween maid and maid may be
More than in sex dividual.

It is a passage that shows my intimate knowledge of female friendship, but it is only a memory, like that of Helena and Hermia in *Midsummer*. There is no more powerful evocation of an idyllic childhood than a time when two innocents love each other more deeply than they would ever love a man. They are, nevertheless, not giving same-sex relationships preference over adult relationships. Emilia and Hippolyta were just completely immersed in each other, as I was with my sister Ambrosia. My adult friendships with my Lady friends, Penelope, Barbara, Elizabeth, and Ursula, were also deeply satisfying, in a more immediate way than with my male friends. At Spa, the Countess of Barlemont and I were a merry pair, shooting on a pistol range and taking tobacco. With men, the focus usually was on the future, not the present. Part of my lifelong dual vision was to keep both perspectives in mind.

*

veryone talks about the House of Tudor, but it was nearly the House of Judley that guided England into the 16th century.

Mother's grandfather Edmund Dudley was a ruthless, unpopular collector of evenues for Henry VII. Many suffered from the grasping hand of Edmund. Henry had rewarded him for keeping the treasury solvent; Edmund was levated to become the second highest power in the land.

dmund's standing relied entirely upon Henry. When Henry VIII ascended, dmund was executed for treason, partly to assuage all the enemies he had made while he extracted revenues. Henry VIII himself was too young to care, nd mostly concerned with securing his own throne. Resentful noblemen who ad had to pay Edmund's tax collectors were the Dudley family's enemies, not Henry.

he family's fortunes subsequently rested upon five-year old John, the rphaned son of a traitor. John became the ward of Sir Edward Guildford. John Judley eventually proved himself in war, becoming Lord Admiral of the Navy fter he helped capture Boulogne. With the title Ward of the Marches he later ut down attacks from Scotland and burned his way through the countryside round Edinburgh. He became one of King Henry VIII's favourites, loyal despite is father's execution.

ohn Dudley sided with Henry VIII at the right time in his divorce and eparation from Rome, and again in the prosecution of Queen Katherine Howard for adultery. Initially, John Dudley was on friendly terms with Henry VIII's daughter Mary, too, even though he was firmly reformist and she was irmly Catholic. John's wife Jane Guildford was also close to Henry VIII's new vife, Catherine Parr. Personal loyalties mattered.

ohn Dudley's life had been one of steady ascendency until he made his fatal misjudgement about the order of succession to the crown. At first things went is way. He became Lord Protector of the young Edward VI after Henry VIII ied.

The sickly Edward himself died in 1553 after a reign of six years, leaving no heir. Before he died, the ailing King Edward chose Lady Jane Grey as his successor. John Dudley, loyal to Edward, was Jane's main supporter.

John was caught on the wrong side, partly as a consequence of miscalculating Mary's intentions. He and most nobles assumed that Mary would not contest the throne. But Mary Tudor was Henry's eldest; in the end, she asserted her rightful claim. Mary promptly bade the Privy Council to execute Lady Jane Grey and those who supported Jane, including her own erstwhile friend John Dudley.

Jane was executed not so much from animosity toward her or her family but more as a warning to anyone who might challenge the legitimacy of the order of succession to the throne. King Philip of Spain supported Queen Mary in her right to the order of succession as the eldest surviving child of King Henry VIII; but later, Philip became the Catholic bogeyman spooking the royal fears that led to so many executions.

When Queen Mary died childless after a reign of four years, my family celebrated because finally the accession of the young Elizabeth promised a prospect of stability. After the Hundred Years War, and the War of the Roses, the Tudors might bring stable government to England. Elizabeth was everyone's hope. The Dudley family again remained loyal when the country was at stake.

Queen Elizabeth's accession to the throne was a great relief to the Protestant cause. Henry had established the Anglican Church, and his son Edward had also been Protestant. But during the five-year rule of Queen Mary, the eldest daughter of Henry VIII, the threat of Catholic Spain loomed over the fate of the nation.

Elizabeth always held the Dudley family dear. All the Tudors could see that the Dudleys could be counted upon for loyalty. Mother's brother Robert, Earl of Leicester, was often at Elizabeth's side; and Elizabeth had christened two of my siblings who had not survived, infant Mary (1556-1558) and little Elizabeth (1560-1567).

According to a pamphlet circulated in 1584, Robert Dudley, Earl of Leicester, my uncle, made his own way ruthlessly in the 1550s, through "plots, treasons, murders, falsehoods, poisonings, lusts, and evil stratagems." Those accusations probably had some truth to them. In a dishonest world, as Machiavelli taught every generation after 1562, honesty and virtue were secondary to preserving order. To me he was just Uncle Robert. Still, the reputation did not escape my notice; the idea that power often comes from evil deeds fed many of my plays. Power and loyalty seemed a fascinating miasma of confusion.

Our family thrived in those years, so close to the throne that we were often swept up by the opposing sides. But QE1 put those sectarian divides to rest. We had some assurance we would be safe as long as she ruled.

Our family was not the equal of the Medici, but it wasn't far off in terms of wealth and extensive influence. Catherine deMedici, who was Queen of France until two years before I was born, had three sons who became kings, attaining an entirely different level of success. The Dudley, Sidney, and Herbert connections were not quite in the royal line but Kings and Queens depended on us, and together we ushered in a great flowering of literature.

The throne was part of our collective identity. I am pleased to say that we also had one of the common traits attributed to the royals: red hair. For over a century, either the King or Queen or both were redheads. Lady Jane Grey was one, and so was I, and some said my temper came from that.

The darker side of that status was that the house of Dudley had a precarious hold on its heritage, without title until 1543; and that scruples were often set aside for my forbears to rise. Fortune's wheel turned quickly. Titles had to be earned by taking the right side, and holding firmly to advantages no matter what it took. The Dudleys were more Machiavellian than Aristotelian. Much of the dark side was rumour I could neither verify nor disprove. The worst of the aspersions stemmed from the unjust legal proceedings that declared my grandfather John and great-grandfather Edmund traitors. We were envied, but envy was not one of my personal faults.

*

My childhood fed my imagination, but it also kept reins upon it, in the sense that I could most easily identify with the inner lives of my peers, the aristocracy. I loved the un-landed working people on the edge of my life, but I saw them from the outside. Perhaps nothing is less understood by the audiences of the 21st century than how much my plays bespeak an abiding comfort with the logic of class divisions. We sat atop a social structure that was stable and that sustained the entirety of the people of England.

I had intimate knowledge both of what the divisions of class meant, and of what they did not mean. Mere ceremony did not make royalty better or superior persons; it did give royalty the weighty responsibility of keeping peace in the kingdom and repelling foreign incursion.

Peasants owned little, but the protective aim of *noblesse oblige* was to allow them to rest easy knowing at least that the court was keeping watch, and that the landed nobility were dispensing care. Nicholas Breton described Wilton as a paradise where "the poor [are] blessedly relieved."

My early life was mostly domestic, the life of a child with her siblings and caretakers, in a busy household with a stream of visitors, entertaining ourselves with stories and music in the evenings and vigorous activity during the day. We divided our time between studies indoors and sports outdoors, riding and archery and lawn bowls. We moved often, between castles and seats of government, with a father who travelled a great deal.

It was a life of privilege, with an attendant sense of *noblesse oblige*. Taking care of our estates was a civic obligation. We felt responsible for those who worked our farms and our domestic lands and estates. We took care that no one went hungry who was in our service. Yes, they must contribute, but there was never a monetary definition of their contributions before the 17th century, when freeholding began to shift under King James. Loyalty mattered more than productivity. When we needed each other, we meant to be there. Our fates were bound together. On a well-run estate, insurrection was unthinkable. Jack Cade sat ill with us.

I think the same principle applies today, in modern, sometimes enlightened, capitalism. Social differences exist with massive disparities in wealth, and labour can be hard, but good leaders are keenly aware of their responsibilities over the economy and public services. The whole idea of the Commonwealth is that the common good is the responsibility of a hierarchy of stakeholders.

With privilege comes an unavoidable uncertainty about the swings of power and influence. Our family knew the exhilaration of power but also the bitterness of envy and the despair of losing not only power but perhaps also your head.

Henry 5 muses on that relationship as he watches soldiers sleeping before a battle. A good leader knows he is no better than others, except in his awesome responsibility for the country as a whole.

> And, but for ceremony, such a wretch,
> Winding up days with toil and nights with sleep,
> Had the fore-hand and vantage of a king.
> The slave, a member of the country's peace,
> Enjoys it; but in gross brain little wots
> What watch the king keeps to maintain the peace,
> Whose hours the peasant best advantages.

A curse on Trump: may his tombstone be written in comic sans. The duty of a sovereign or a president is indeed to take care of the upper classes, the infrastructure of the economy. He only took care of a few cronies, not the power core. Not even in religion, the military, and the City. He made use of them all but afforded them no protection, no profit. Couldn't even pass major bills for business.

Thus my final words are a curse, from the high dignity of a never unentitled Dowager Countess.

*

Forgive me, dear Reader, I'm a man, disguising himself not just as a woman but moreover as a woman who is the pinnacle of what it means to be human, according to Harold Bloom. If this work is an appropriation, let it be an appropriation of that, of the common ground of all gendered and acculturated variations.

Almost everything in this account has a basis in recorded fact, though the only quantum computer is my brain. I have taken the liberty of projecting a fictional gender because that is the very thing that Mary Sidney did, writing plays in the voices of both genders.

Only a double vision could even have comprehended that feat of legerdemain, the universal in the particular gender. In the plays attributed to WS, a sometimes unseen but steady force often lies with women. There is a female stamp upon the plays that is incontrovertible once you begin looking for it. How could it not be a woman?

There are over a hundred women with speaking parts in the three-dozen "Stratford" Canon. Though outnumbered, female characters sway the plot and the rhetoric. Many of the plots have at the core the issue of lawful marriage. Contingent on marriage are the acquisition of wealth, the legitimacy of power, the settlement of treaties, the noble qualities inherited, and of course the impulses of lust and love. Women hold sway in these plays from the margins. Without them, most plays would not just be poorer they would also lack a core dramatic narrative. Men often launch into solo ventures; always, their connections to women pull the play into balance.

That subtext is consistent from the first play Two Gentlemen of Verona to the last play Two Noble Kinsmen. The titles are not a coincidence; they are a clear irony. In those two plays two best friends bicker with each other as they contest the love of the same woman, without bothering to consult her. There is little to be seen of nobility in the title characters. On the surface, both plays follow the story arc of the rival friends, but the women's stories are presented vividly, not as after-thoughts.

The former play distinguishes between love and lust. Lust drives the plot but love pulls it back into balance.

The latter play is a critique of war and of male codes of chivalry, a critique often articulated not by the men themselves but by its female characters, by the mourning queens, Emilia, and the Gaoler's daughter. What a perfect example of the way the subtext arises in the plays; we must first follow the main plot but must also be alert to clues about what marginalized female characters think and what they aspire to. Contests drive the plot but women pull men back into issues of caring.

*

In terms of rhetoric, women's vulnerability prompts them to weigh words carefully as they face choices and outcomes. The men often seem wooden and bombastic, ill-attuned to the nuances of decisions.

What quickly becomes clear is that a sense of purpose defines genders. Female characters are capable of resolve, one of the Bard's favourite words, suggesting the actions of solving problems and making effective responses. "Resolve" is the capacity "to untie; to answer, solve; to decide, determine."[5]

Female characters often function as loosening forces to disentangle knots in the plots. As Carol Neely Thomas says, one of the patterns in the festive comedies is "to break down resistance and to release desire and affection."[6] Going one step further, tragedies complement the comedies, representing failures to untangle resistant knots.

Another of the Bard's favourite words that applies to women is "will:"[7] female characters across genres make reasoned, heartfelt decisions, clear in their minds about their purposes. Indeed, it seems they must be clear in their minds to survive and thrive, limited as they are in their license to exercise any choices at all.

In contrast, male characters, especially the early ones, have ample room to make decisions yet lack purposefulness, shifting with the tides of emotions and events. Most often, they tangle the knots that they and the female characters must attempt to untie. By mid-career the Bard looks for a more balanced

---

Oxford English Dictionary "Resolve" def. 16 and 17. : 1591 H. Smith Treat. Lords Supper i. 26 "Resolue this not & al is cleere." 1550 T. Cranmer Def. Sacrament iv. f. 94 "S. Augustine, most plainly resolueth this matter in his booke.., disputing against two kinds of heretiques."

Neely, Carol Thomas. *Broken Nuptials in Shakespeare's Plays,* Yale University Press, New Haven, 1985, p.40.

Ibid. "Will" def. 5 and 6. "The action of willing or choosing to do something; the movement or attitude of the mind which is directed with conscious intention to (and, normally, issues immediately in) some action, physical or mental; volition."

approach, exploring the idea that men's flexibility and indefiniteness can also in many ways count as strengths: they can take risks to refashion and rationalize their goals to suit the exigencies of the moment; however, those risks put their purposes in jeopardy, making their strengths momentary.

*

Come now, make your own lists: are there not a larger number of fully-fledged women than men? You can count on one hand the great but terribly troubled men: Hamlet, who often seems adolescent rather than fully mature; Othello, whose warped imagination is badly deceived, as is that of the gullible Titus; and Lear, who like Richard II fully understands the immensity of his fall. Only two retain a full measure of dignity and nobility, Henry 5 and Prospero, but those two should not be taken as the norm. Excepting those two, all of the great men fall, whereas women such as Portia, Olivia, Rosalind, Isabella, and Hermione soar, willing their way to live, to accommodate, to heal and join. Even the tragic female victims such as Desdemona and Cordelia assert their worth and when they fall as victims the fingers point at the tragic failure of the male 'heroes.' Cleopatra too makes a more triumphant statement than any Roman emperor; she has the fifth act entirely to herself.

The Bard's view of women went against a documented bias that judged women to be easily swayed by their biological needs and their emotions, whereas men were assumed to be capable of deliberate restraint and reasoned action.

The history of ideas often hinges on reactions to something immediate. In Elizabethan times there was a specific event that might have prompted such a reaction in Mary Sidney.

The "Homily on Marriage", read out in English churches from 1562 on, said "For the woman is a weake creature, not indued with like strength and constancie of minde ∙∙∙more various in fantasies and opinions ∙∙∙more prone to all weak affections and dispositions of mind."[8]

What would the Bard have been thinking as those words were read out weekly, from her infancy onward? The plays contradict the homily. Women do indeed have "strength and constancy of mind" from the very first plays forward; and the portraits of men seem designed to show the variability in their affections and the illogic in their reasoning.

---

[8] Evans, Malcolm. "Truth's True Contents: Goodnight Ladies" in *Signifying Nothing* (1986), p.175.

Powerful women such as Portia, Rosalind, Venus, Viola, Margaret in the Henry 6 plays and Cleopatra stand firm, not relinquishing their capacity to choose, albeit within conventional restraints. Juliet also belongs in that troupe for defying her father, daring to take what might be poison, and ending her own life because that is all she owns, the same decision made by Lucrece and Cleopatra. Cordelia and Desdemona are also undiminished by their tragic fates. These are magnificent women, stronger than the general run of men in the plays, nearly the equals of the strongest such as Henry 5, Brutus, and Prospero.

*

Back to grief. It is the most human of emotions, more than love, parenthood, pride, all the levels of self-fulfillment. Grief in its simplest form is the primitive observation that something is missing when a body loses life. The body remains, but something else has gone. That observation is the foundation of all religion. And that sense of a spirit flown is the foundation of all great literature. Philip Sidney's departure was lofted gloriously upon the words of Mary Sidney, Countess of Pembroke.

By Tom Dlugosch

Recommended Reading

Faulkes, Fred. *Tiger's Heart in Woman's Hide*. Trafford, 2007.

Hannay, Margaret P. *Philip's Phoenix: Mary Sidney, Countess of Pembroke*. Oxford University Press, 1990.

Hannay, Margaret P. *Selected Works of Mary Sidney Herbert, Countess of Pembroke*. Arizona Center for Medieval and Renaissance Studies, 2005.

Robinson, John Martin. *Wilton House the Art, Architecture and Interiors of One of Britain's Great Stately Homes*. Rizzoli Electa, 2021.

Sidney, Philip, and Mary Sidney Pembroke. *The Sidney Psalter the Psalms of Sir Philip and Mary Sidney*. Oxford University Press, 2009.

Vendler, Helen Hennessy. *The Art of Shakespeare's Sonnets*. Belknap Press, 1999.

Williams, Robin. *Sweet Swan of Avon: Did a Woman Write Shakespeare?* Wilton Circle Press, 2019.

Printed in Great Britain
by Amazon

42124352R00076